Beautifully and wholehearte ... tricia invites
the reader to witness her batt ... *rple Dragon.*
Her words have the energy to ... ..umanity. Patricia is
a healer, even though she's in ...…aing herself. *Yollanda Olavarria-DeMarco, United States*

Reading Patricia's book has awakened the dragon-fighter in me, and I now know that I can get through the challenges of treatment and recovery. *Heath L Silberfeld, diagnosed with breast cancer, United States*

The Grace, dignity, and joy Patricia exudes during this tumultuous journey render me so very humble. She makes veterans like me look feeble! Her attitude and mindset are essential! Such strength, humor, and genuine goodness! Thank you for showing us how to endure challenges while loving life so deeply. *Lori Odorizzi Bari, LMS survivor, United States*

I admire the honesty, strength, vulnerability, and courage Patricia displays as she writes and shares her journey. Her wisdom is guiding her. True happiness is in the little moments, like in the ones she has created and shared with others. You are a star Patricia! Remain true to your love for life. *Fabiana Mello, England*

Patricia colors life, and this color comes from inside her. *Cida Madeiro, MD, Brazil*

The transparency, strength, and above all, courage to share her journey, confirm the determination that has guided Patricia's life. Her soul is noble, beautiful, and illuminated. Thanks for the life lessons. God chooses those who, even in the hardest moments, remain strong, searching for more strength and light, believing in both medical and spiritual treatments, independently of faith. *Elônia Magalhães, Brazil*

I find myself in awe of Patricia's ability to accept and face all she is going through. I've witnessed her spiritual evolution. *Maria Araujo, Portugal*

During the most arduous time, Patricia has brought color to the lives of so many. What a beautiful example! She is light, color, and needed here on Earth. *Duarte Miranda, Brazil*

I have never seen a person with so much strength as she battles cancer. Patricia inspires us, make us see the world differently, and give us strength. Reading her journey has been my daily inspiration. *Juliana Azoubel, breast cancer survivor, Brazil*

Patricia is a beautiful soul and has such a wonderful outlook and attitude. She is a true inspiration to so many. *Helen Elizabeth, LMS survivor, United States*

Patricia's experience has touched and humbled me, and so many others. Her strength, courage, and determination to fight the dragon are inspiring. Purple is the color of hope. *Rachel B Sellers, United States*

Thank you Patricia for the life lessons you have been teaching us. You demonstrate strength, courage, and perseverance Patricia. *Jacquline Calaça, leukemia survivor, Brazil*

Witnessing Patricia's journey has been a gift to my soul. Her courage to accept the unexpected, to confront the uncertain, to embrace vulnerability, and also her gratitude for all she has, are the perfect example of her choice to live a wholehearted life. Day after day she dares! *Ana Cusi, Argentina*

You transmit force to us Patricia, while you teach that it is worth fighting for life, always, despite the adversities in our way. Thank you. *Karla Padilla, Brazil*

While facing my own troubles, I hear you Patricia, and your words give me strength to move forward. I have profound admiration for your great energy, and for your faith and courage. *Sandra Tenorio, Brazil*

Patricia's spirit shines like a star! *Belisa Sherman, LMS survivor, United States*

It impresses me the way Patricia has embraced her cancer and she is appreciating this world and universe in a way like none other. She is one of the strongest women I have ever known. *Kim Chamberlain, United States*

My Journey with the Purple Dragon

Living with Leiomyosarcoma, a Rare and Aggressive Cancer

PATRICIA MOREIRA-CALI

BALBOA.
PRESS

A DIVISION OF HAY HOUSE

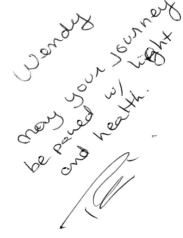

Wendy
may your journey
be paved w/ light
and health.

Balboa Press books may be ordered through booksellers or by contacting:

Balboa Press
A Division of Hay House
1663 Liberty Drive
Bloomington, IN 47403
www.balboapress.com
1 (877) 407-4847

Because of the dynamic nature of the Internet, any web addresses or links contained in this book may have changed since publication and may no longer be valid. The views expressed in this work are solely those of the author and do not necessarily reflect the views of the publisher, and the publisher hereby disclaims any responsibility for them.

The author of this book does not dispense medical advice or prescribe the use of any technique as a form of treatment for physical, emotional, or medical problems without the advice of a physician, either directly or indirectly. The intent of the author is only to offer information of a general nature to help you in your quest for emotional and spiritual well-being. In the event you use any of the information in this book for yourself, which is your constitutional right, the author and the publisher assume no responsibility for your actions.

Any people depicted in stock imagery provided by Thinkstock are models, and such images are being used for illustrative purposes only. Certain stock imagery © Thinkstock.

Printed in the United States of America.

ISBN: 978-1-4525-1757-5 (sc)
ISBN: 978-1-4525-1759-9 (hc)
ISBN: 978-1-4525-1758-2 (e)

Library of Congress Control Number: 2014912393

Balboa Press rev. date: 11/24/2014

FOREWORD

I met Patricia at meditation group. During a break, she was sipping tea and I was waiting to use restroom. We shared a smile and I spoke to myself out loud, something about *the journalist in me*. Her eyes widened.

"You're a writer? I am in search of a writer. Actually an editor."

And so our friendship began. Over a number of lunches and coffees, I realized Patricia didn't need a writer so much as someone to help organize and edit her journals of healing from a rare form of cancer. With the help of typist extraordinaire Jessica Miller, we three pieced together a slice of Patricia's life (from diagnosis to chemotherapy and one year anniversary) that is nothing less than extraordinary.

Whether or not you believe in the healing capabilities of gurus, entities, or past life regression, whether you're a follower of Spiritism, Buddhism, Christianity, or any other practice, whether you are an agonist or an atheist, your belief system is irrelevant. Patricia's story is one of survival, a search for hope, and a release of the past to embrace a fearless future.

I am so fortunate to have met Patricia and proud to call her my friend. She has reminded me every single day that we all have the power within ourselves to heal what ails us. We each need to believe in ourselves and in the truth that we seek out. That's when we will truly be set free – when we find peace within.

- Jennifer Grant, April 23, 2014

PREFACE

The courage to make public my journey with The Dragon (Leiomyosarcoma), as recorded in a journal I kept since July 2013, did not come easily. My words were written to myself (my soul) and to the invisible audience around all (the invisible world and beings), as I came to realize later. But once Jennifer Grant insisted that they could help others going through their own journeys with cancer or other hardships, I surrendered to the fear of being judged for having taken *unconventional detours* along the conventional road of grieving and towards healing.

These are the words of MY own path. The places I went and the experiences I lived are the result of me finally listening to my own voice, my intuition, which went from being whispered softly in my ears to firmly screaming in my heart and soul. With difficulty at first, I tuned away from my conscious, rational, and analytical mind, and followed my gut instinct, my intuition, the feelings derived from the deepest perception of my soul and the Universe.

On my path, there were just too many "*weird coincidences*" to be ignored, making it easier for me to just dive in and go explore *the unknown*, without rationalizing my decisions. I soon learned that there are no coincidences in life; I learned that I seem to have a distinctive perception of what is around me, at times hearing with more than my ears, and seeing with more than my eyes; I appear to connect with *the energy* around, "*scanning*" what surrounds me with great curiosity, perhaps perceiving just a little more than most would, although everyone has this innate ability. The end result of increased awareness is more "synchronicity" and "channeling," which lead to what we call "coincidences." I now accept the premonition dreams I have had, the "odd" encounters throughout the small villages of remote areas of the world, and my "guessing" as part of who my true self really is; I am now okay with my own being, without need to whisper my truth in my sister's ears while asking for secrecy. No embarrassment. No fear of being poorly judged or ridiculed. I accept my own truth and finally can embrace it as part of who I truly am as a spiritual being having a human experience. I know now that my body, mind, and soul coexist, but they are not the same.

Yes, I have a diagnosis of a voracious cancer, the dragon called Leiomyosarcoma (LMS), but this fact does not define me as a person. This is a medical condition my physical body has, but it cannot sicken my spirit. I am who I am as a person, as a soul. I am my actions, my smiles, my tears, my feelings, and my true being.

I hope that sharing my steps towards healing, from fear to peace, from tears to smiles, from feeling stuck to moving forward with The Dragon, enlightens you, even if in a small way.

With desire of health and peace within all,

Patricia

P.S. *Please take into consideration that I am not a professional writer; I am just a woman, a mother, a dietitian, and a human being diagnosed with cancer, sharing her thoughts and feelings while on her healing path.*

"A human being is a part of the whole that we call the universe, a part limited in time and space. He experiences himself, his thoughts and feelings, as something separated from the rest – a kind of optical illusion of his consciousness. This illusion is a prison for us, restricting us to our personal desires and to affection for only the few people nearest us. Our task must be to free ourselves from this prison by embrace of all living being and all of natures." — Albert Einstein

(This powerful quote was written on a painting hung on the wall by the table I sat at a café, before heading to the airport in Orlando, to fly to Abadiânia, Brazil, on July 28, 2013. It touched me then, and its meaning has stayed with me.)

"Don't be intimidated by other people's opinions. Only mediocrity is sure of itself, so take risks and do what you really want to do." — Paulo Coelho, *Aleph*

JULY 29, 2013 - FLYING FROM HOME TO ABADIÂNIA, BRAZIL

I had never heard of Abadiânia until a couple of weeks ago. I don't know anyone there, and I'm not sure what exactly I will do there, or what will happen. But I am going, flowing with the cascade of events that started... When exactly did it all start? Two weeks ago? Three months ago? A year, twenty-five years, or maybe an eternity ago? I truly don't know.

The coincidences or happenings that have led me to be seated on this plane, flying to encounter the unknown, have kept me swirling, both physically and emotionally, during the past fourteen months, and especially during the last three. My beliefs have been shaken, and I have chosen to allow myself to embark on a journey through territories somewhat out of my comfort zone.

Where should I start telling this tale? To make some sense, I hope, I will start with the most pertinent and recent events.

1

"Never ignore warning signals in your body, even the smallest ones. It doesn't matter the experience of others if your intuition whispers that something isn't as it should be." — Patricia Moreira-Cali

THE CATALYST: AN UNEXPECTED DIAGNOSIS

November 2012 – The Routine Checkup

I usually have my annual gynecologic exam in August. But in 2012, I didn't see my doctor until November. As usual, my mammogram was normal. I reported that my migraines and insomnia were managed with treatment, and all else seemed fine. The doctor proceeded to do a PAP smear. With the exam complete, I felt an urge to ask:

"Is it part of pre-menopause to have bloating and periods which last longer?"

"How long?" my doctor asked.

I told her "between 4 to 12 days" and that "my friends already in menopause say that this type of change is normal".

My doctor gave me an inquisitive look. "Not necessarily normal. Let's go to the Ultrasound room to take a look."

The ultrasound reviewed two fibroids – one the size of an orange, the other a lemon. I offered information that my mother and two sisters had so many fibroids that none of them have uteruses anymore. The doctor proceeded to tell me that uterine masses are usually benign, but she would like to repeat the ultrasound in one month, just to make sure.

Hmm! I was right to suspect that there was something not right. I should have listened to my own body's signals.

December 2012 - Good News: No Growth of Fibroids

After the ultrasound, Dr. R says: "That's very good! No growth on the fibroids." I rejoice, relieved. She goes on to say: "But just to make sure, I'd like to repeat the test again in two more months." I agree, without much worry, and life goes on.

March 2013 – Not So Good News: Gray Area Growth of One Fibroid

I head to the gynecologist's office for the third ultrasound, carelessly saying, "Here I go, to make sure my orange didn't turn into a grapefruit." I'm referring to the bigger fibroid.

"The large one has grown some," says the doctor. "Its growth is in a gray area, not so much that I'm very concerned, but not so little that I'm comfortable."

We discuss options: surgery or waiting a little longer. I have a trip scheduled in two weeks for my mother's 80th birthday in Brazil. The doctor advises me that I can go, but I must return for another ultrasound the day after I arrive back.

Arriving home, I share the not-so-good news with my 17-year-old son and my husband.

"What is more important: to go to your Mom's birthday or to find out if you have cancer?" My son's question takes me by surprise and I respond: "Gosh, Yannick! I do not have cancer. Your grandma lives far away, and she will be eighty only once. We don't know how many more years she has. So, I do the test when I come back."

But his question stays with me, and the next day I ask my primary physician for her opinion.

"If you are going to be worried when you are gone, why don't you have the surgery right away and go?"

I call the gynecologist's office immediately and the nurse says, "I'll talk to the doctor but if she said you can travel, it's because she believes you can wait."

The nurse calls back and tells me the doctor says I can travel without worrying. Everyone I encounter reassures me, "No big deal. I had many fibroids," or "Lots of women have them," or "My sister, my friend, my mom, my neighbor had five, ten, fifteen," et cetera. Somehow, I am still not completely at ease.

March 20, 2013 – To Brazil I Go, to Celebrate My Mother

So to Brazil we went and we celebrated my Mom's 80th birthday, giving her two surprise parties and loads of happiness. I felt she needed to feel special, celebrated, after a life of great emotional suffering. I also got to see about a hundred family members. Unlike me, Brazilians usually don't move. They tend to live in the same city all their lives. I have lived in the USA for 30 years... an unusual bird.

We also had time to head to the beach house for some delightful lazy days. The coconut trees, the breeze, the blue ocean, all so enchanting! Most of the time I was carefree, just enjoying life with family. However, from time to time the subject of the "fibroids" would come up, and all reassured me that there wasn't anything for me to be concerned about, since fibroids are so common. "Hum. Why do my instincts insist in murmuring doubts in my ears?" I wonder.

I made the most of my time in Brazil, and as I left I believed it was worth having made the trip for my Mother. But, I can't deny that even though everyone insisted that the "fibroids" and possible surgery were absolutely nothing to worry about, and I tried to believe them, there was a faint but persistent little voice within making me fell uneasy, from the time I left on the trip and until now during my return.

Carefree in Brazil, with my mother and children, and time on my own, unaware that The Dragon had already entered my body.

April 1, 2013 - April's Fool Day Brought Me No Joke

I arrive back on a Monday, and I have the fourth ultrasound. So, on April's Fools Day, I get the news that more growth is detected on the large fibroid, and right then we scheduled the robotic surgery.

Again, everyone insists it's nothing to be concerned about, but I can't help but to feel doubt, uneasiness within.

April 17, 2013 – Robotic Surgery

On April 17, I am at the hospital, about to have a total hysterectomy, uterus and ovaries removed, and I jokingly tell the anesthesiologist, "Just make sure I wake up, okay?" That was my only concern at the time.

Hours later I wake up, full of energy, feeling good. My sister and best friend Andrea has come from Brazil to be with me and stays at the hospital overnight. The next morning I am discharged and started what was to be a speedy recovery.

"When we least expect it, life sets us a challenge to test our courage and willingness to change; at such a moment, there is no point in pretending that nothing has happened or in saying that we are not yet ready. The challenge will not wait. Life does not look back." — Paulo Coelho

APRIL 23, 2013: AND FROM THIS DAY ON MY LIFE CHANGES FOREVER. I AM INTRODUCED TO THE PURPLE DRAGON.

I was to have a follow-up two weeks after the surgery, but I get a call to go to see the doctor today, just six days after the surgery. *Hmm*, I thought, but again, my family tells me, "There is nothing to be concerned about. You probably got the appointment date wrong."

My husband John stay in the waiting room. The nurse takes me in, still walking slowly. I sit and wait. The doctor comes in, sits, asks how I am doing and then....

"Sorry. It was a tumor," she finally says.

"What?" I ask confused.

"Yes, it was cancer."

I go instantly numb, and the blood leaves my face. I feel strange, like in a fog.

"Which type?" I ask, on a monotone and faint voice, still in disbelief but hoping it would be a carcinoma.

"The bad, aggressive one," the doctor replies. "Leiomyosarcoma, a very rare type of cancer." This is the first time I've ever heard of Leiomyosarcoma (LMS), but I know sarcomas are the aggressive type of cancer. I ask about which treatment I should have.

"The only treatment available, you already had: surgery. I am sending you to an oncologist for you to be followed and have further tests."

"If I already had the treatment and it is all out, why do I need further tests and an oncologist?" I ask.

"This type of tumor likes to travel to the lungs and liver, but I took it all out in one piece and we caught it early, in stage 1. You have a good chance."

"CANCER. AGGRESSIVE. TRAVEL. NO TREATMENT. CHANCE." My mind spins. I feel clumsy and numb, as if I had just entered a dark room with no exit doors, no windows, no light. It's cold here, helpless, lifeless, just like I feel inside. A tear rolls down my cheek and I plead with the doctor, "Please get my husband and my sister."

"You're not going to faint on me are you?" she asks, looking at my pale face.

I nod and stay still. Time passes very slowly. When they enter the room, I say THE DREADED WORDS for the first time: "I HAVE CANCER AND IT IS THE WORST TYPE."

I knew at that moment that my life would never be the same. I passed through a door and entered a new cold space from where there would never be a true exit or way to escape. An aggressive intruder has busted into my body, my life.

Where did my freedom go? Where are my dreams of growing older and of holding my grandkids someday? Where is the healthy body within my thin frame? I am silent on the drive home. I am still numb, in a dense fog.

Arriving at home, I share the news, monotone. My family is in shock, too, I imagine, but they try to be reassuring for my sake, repeating that I'm going to be fine since the cancer was removed. However, I'm in the medical field and I know too much to be at peace. Uncertainty, uncertainty, and more uncertainty lie ahead, and there is nothing I can do about it.

My best friends come by. They hug me, comfort me as the tears of dread and sorrow roll down my face, and say I won't be alone on the journey ahead, and that they will be by my side. They tell me now is time for me to take care of myself and accept to be cared for;

to stop trying to save all the poor sick kids of the world; to care less about my patients and more myself. I just listen, just listen, and cry.

I take to my bed. I don't want to open my eyes. I don't want to hear. I don't want to speak. I don't want to eat. I don't want to think, but the scary thoughts keep creeping in, over and over again. The tears flow down constantly like an endless stream. I can't sleep. My core is shaken and I know the course of my life has shifted towards the unknown.

April 25, 2013 – The First Oncologist appointment of Many (Forever) Ones

Two days later I see the oncologist, who happens to be a Brazilian friend. The tears keep on flowing as he tells me the "good" news first:

"It was caught at Stage 1, which is extremely rare with LMS. Most find out when it has already spread."

Now on to the bad news: "LMS is a very aggressive cancer, which usually spreads to the lungs or other bloody soft tissues, like the liver, or spinal cord. There are three grades of aggressiveness, and yours is grade 2 (later to be diagnosed as 3, the most aggressive). There are no radiation or chemotherapy protocols for stage 1, so surgery to remove tumors as they appear is the treatment."

Moving on to more bad news: "Since LMS is so rare (1 in 5 million has it), there isn't a lot of research on this type of cancer and there is no blood test to detect it. So, we will do CT-scans (like having 300 x-rays each time) for surveillance, every three months for three years, when it is more likely to re-appear, and every six months for another two years. From then on, once per year."

"There aren't many studies, but statistics points toward you having 50-75 percent chance of survival in five years. LMS is more likely to show back up in the first two to three years following diagnosis."

"What can I do?" I ask, desperate to be proactive, to be able to DO something to increase my chance of survival. I get the answer I was to hear over and over from all oncologists I saw: "*Be positive.*"

That's it? Be positive? That is not enough and besides, how do I do that, be positive with this scary, gloomy, and hopeless news coming at me out of nowhere?

In a desperate attempt to be able to do something, *anything,* I stupidly ask, "I am a vegetarian. Should I start eating meat?" Yes, that's how desperate I am to do something. I am a dietitian, I know the answer, but I need something to do, to hold on to. Just as I teach my patients to change their diets to improve their health, I want it to be this simple for me, too.

"No. Continue to be a vegetarian. I wish most of my patients could be vegetarians. Unfortunately, the only thing you can do is be positive, try to go on with your life."

I want to be proactive, make something positive happen, make this prognosis go away, far away from my life. But again, all I can do is be positive, but no recipe for positivism is handed to me. I leave the office feeling powerless. How do I begin to be anything other than just plain afraid, sad, and helpless?

April 24-30, 2013 – Time of Deep Grieving

The days that followed were sad, very sad, blue, and scary. I don't remember getting angry, although out loud I would say, "Why me? Why?"

My loved ones kept pushing me to get out of my puddle of tears. I asked for time; I needed to grieve the loss of my good health and get used to the reality of an uncertain future.

"You need to work less and not make exceptions to help your patients," I am told. "You need to take better care of yourself," and "You need to worry less about helping others and start to focus on yourself, on putting yourself first."

"I'll put myself first," I promise, knowing how hard that would be.

Contemplating life and its meaning after surgery and diagnosis of cancer.

"Meditation takes our mind beyond our mental patterns and history of conditioning to a state of purity where we can relate to our inner guidance." — Deepak Chopra

MEDITATION AND RELAXATION FOR ACCEPTANCE AND HEALING

I search for, find, and start to listen to guided relaxation and meditation apps on my cellular phone, and I return to Sunday meditation at a local Tibetan Buddhist Center.

At this point in time, it is very hard to find calm on my own, as anxiety, fear, and sadness, easily invade my mind. Guided meditation doesn't require effort, as it basically walks me through the path to replace distress and balance my negative emotions, inviting peace and calm within.

Diving into stillness is so helpful to me, as it takes me away, even if just for a little while. Actually, I don't want to do anything else but hear reassuring and soothing words, revealing a field of pure potentially, even for perfect health. So many nights are spent with headphones on, listening to Glenn Harold, until my body and mind finally succumb and rest. Later I discovered Deepak Chopra, Louise Hay, Wayne Dyer, and so many others, all with guided meditation, and even audio books, free on YouTube.

May 3, 2013 – Sarcoma Center and My Sister Goes Back Home

My oncologist encouraged me to make an appointment at a sarcoma center, as most oncologists see very few cases of sarcoma yearly. Sarcomas account for only 1% of all types of cancers. I went for a second opinion from the sarcoma team at the Moffitt Cancer Center in Tampa, Florida, only to hear again that I was lucky the cancer was caught in stage 1, that my gynecologist did a great job as a surgeon, and that the only thing I could do was "just be positive."

My sister and husband tell me, "See, that's good."

"Good?" Inside, in silence, I screamed, "What is good? The diagnosis, the prognosis and the no treatment reality are all still here, rooted inside my body, my soul. How is that good exactly?" But I didn't say much. I just cried silently, inside, as we drove to take my sister to the airport in Orlando, knowing I'd miss her terribly.

We drop her off, and as we drive away tears of sorrow flow. John says, "From now on, no more tears, right? You need to start smiling."

How could he say that? My tears are my companions. They help to wash away some of the helpless feeling, the pain, the fear.

I cry more. I don't know how to begin to be positive, to be myself again.

May 4, 2013 – Still Haven't Shared The Dragon News

Wanting to spare my Mom the pain of my diagnosis, I have not shared it with family and friends in Brazil.

The day before my sister left we went to the nondenominational chapel alongside Lake Alice. I sat in silence, in a meditative state, at times a little numb. Now I find myself posting a picture of it on Facebook, writing "Light... An amazing place to contemplate LIFE, its meaning, its surprise." I do not mention my diagnosis

"I keep dreaming of a future with a long and healthy life, not lived in the shadow of cancer but in the light." — Patrick Swayze

BACK TO WORK, TRYING TO ADD SOME NORMALCY IN MY NEW LIFE... NOT EASY

On May 13, I go back to work, for just a few hours per day. On the third day, I'm with a patient when my assistant calls me. "There's a call from the Moffitt Sarcoma Team. It's a nurse."

"The LMS grade is actually 3 out of 3 and you need to see a clinical oncologist to discuss treatment right away." I'm so shocked with the news that I weep.

"Which treatment? I thought there was no treatment?"

"That is for you to discuss with the clinical oncologist. Maybe chemo."

I apologize to my patient, but I can't think, concentrate, or work. I go home in tears. How and when can I have normalcy in my life? This cancer diagnosis is overtaking my life. I want my freedom and health back.

I have an appointment with my oncologist this same day. He tells me he agrees that the news wasn't given to me the right way, and although it was surprising that the grade is now 3, that would not change the course of action at this point. I am then referred to Mayo Clinic sarcoma treatment center in Jacksonville, Florida to get established as a patient, as I had decided not to go back to Moffitt. I'm starting to make decisions about what feels right or wrong, to become the CEO of my care team.

May 16, 2013 – Third Opinion at Mayo Clinic, Jacksonville, Florida

My husband is in Europe when the appointment day arrives. Luckily a good friend and scientist, Gideon, comes with me to help process all the information. Amanda, my lovely daughter, is also there for support. The doctor is very approachable, knowledgeable, and talkative. He searches for information and statistics on LMS stage 1. He finds one single and small study with a chemotherapy protocol, which shows no effectiveness. Half the women died, chemo or no chemo. He finds a website where he enters my personal information and a prognosis is given. Now I'm told that my estimated survival rate is 57% in 5 years. That is much worse than the 75% given before.

Now I have a great new sarcoma oncologist, and dooming news. I look down and cry. Amanda holds me and says "Mom. That is not going to be for you. You are going to be fine. Remember you need to be positive."

Yes, the prescription again was to be freaking positive, nothing else. That sucks!

We leave the clinic with tons of information, including the lack of studies. I'm not hungry, but I need to eat. I have lost weight since the diagnosis, as my appetite isn't good at all. During lunch and the drive home to Gainesville, all I think about are the darn statistics: 57% alive, 43% dead in 5 years. My friend Gideon tries to encourage me. I can't say much. I am so sad, discouraged, and scared.

"Every individual matters. Every individual has a role to play. Every individual makes a difference." — Jane Goodall

OPENING UP ABOUT THE CANCER AND REACHING OUT FOR SUPPORT: EXTREMELY ESSENTIAL

It was when I was ready to take my puppy for a short walk for the first time in a while that a neighbor stopped her car and asked what exactly I had been diagnosed with. I shared the news.

"Honey, do not go through this alone, as I did over thirty years ago when I was diagnosed with breast cancer. Tell everybody and you will see: Some people will disappear from your life, but others will be coming out of the woodwork to help you."

I wasn't sure if I was ready to tell everybody, but it was nice talking to someone who had been there, who could relate to what I was going through.

That night, even with the guided relaxation apps, I couldn't sleep. John had left for Europe, my sister for Brazil, Amanda for Jacksonville. It was midnight, and thinking of my neighbor's advice, I wrote on Facebook, *"Sarcomas are only 1% of all cancers. There are many faces of leiomyosarcoma. I'm one of them."* I felt both relief and guilt, as I didn't want to burden others with my gloomy news. I feared someone in Brazil might see what was happening and would tell my mother. I still wanted to spare her any emotional distress. But who will know what leiomyosarcoma is?

I turned off the computer. At 1:00 a.m., I turned it back on to send a message with a burning question to a "guru" I had met in Bali one year before. To my surprise, there were several supportive messages from everywhere, in response to my post. I cried like a baby as I read aloud a Bahamian prayer a student of mine, from years ago, sent me. I slept like an angel afterward. My neighbor had done me an enormous favor, and she was so right that I needed to share, to open up, not to deal with it all alone. Actually, on that night I decided that the more people knew the better, in the hopes that my story could alert and possibly save others about getting checkups and following their intuition.

My neighbor Jane also told me, "We have a neighbor who you should meet. I think you two will get along, but let me ask her first if I can give you her number."

May 29, 2013 – Support Starts to Flow from Different Parts of the World

An ex-student of mine writes a message from India. It touches my heart. It said:

"I have known you for a few years, and I know you as a very positive, powerful woman and a fighting spirit. You WILL get through this, and you will be cured. My prayers, wishes, and faith are always with you. There is a quote in the Bhagavad Gita (our holy book), "The power of God is with you at all times: through the activities of mind, senses, breathing, and emotions; and it is constantly doing all the work using you as a mere instrument." I really cherish knowing you. Lots of love… Sohini."

Another student from 10 years ago, writes, " Patricia, you are a truly beautiful human being with the most sparkling soul. You share selflessly with this world, and I'm honored to know you and your genuine heart. All of the strength that you've given to others is with you as you persevere. Know that you're in my thoughts, my prayers, and my heart. I'm sending you beams of love and light. Love you always, Nicoletta."

Messages like these brought tears to my eyes and warmth to my heart. I felt less alone, and I decided that I'd continue to share my journey with anyone wanting to be part of it.

"Sometimes coincidence is a plan in disguise." — *Unknown*

LET THE COINCIDENCES UNLEASH

June 1, 2013 – "Coincidences" Abound and I Am Introduced to the Unknown

I rarely go downtown, but back in April, some days after my diagnosis, I went for coffee with my sister, husband, and puppy to relieve them from the heavy burden of my doom and gloom. I was certain I would not meet anyone and opted for a local café instead of Starbucks. Well, on the first table over there's a doctor I have known for a long time, but who I haven't seen in years. He has had leukemia for years. I didn't say anything about my diagnosis, and after the hello to him and his wife I said goodbye. I got his number, as I had thought of contacting him just the day before, but even after the encounter, I didn't call.

Three days later he calls me asking if anything was going on, and sobbing, I told him the news and asked, "How do you do it?"

He was very comforting, and I knew he knew exactly how helpless and lost I felt.

Fast forward to now, a Saturday in May, and I am on his porch having coffee, being supported, and encouraged to go to the biggest cancer center in the world, MD Anderson, in Houston, Texas. I say I'll consider, but I feel comfortable with three opinions already. (Later on I took his advice). Saturday morning coffee at the Jaffe's become a ritual I came to appreciate and treasure.

That evening, at the same local café downtown, another unexpected encounter happened. Cris, a long time friend I haven't seen in a few years, arrives and sits on the table next to ours. I share my diagnosis news and she immediately says "Of course, it had to be a rare type. You are very special so you can't have what everybody has. It came and it is already gone. Come by my place so I can do some healing Reike on you." I agreed that I would call soon, without telling her I didn't know what Reike was.

June 6-10, 2013 – John of God Appears on My Radar

It's then that I get an unexpected email from a cousin who lives in London, suggesting that I look up Louise Hay for meditation, as well as a healer in Brazil called John of God (João de Deus). I've never heard of either one. I thank her, saying I was going to look them up, but I ended up forgetting and I didn't.

I get another unexpected email from a dear friend on the other coast in California, suggesting that I "consider looking into a healer in Brazil, John of God." I thank her, mention it to my agnostic husband (who rolls his eyes), and say I'll look into it, but I didn't.

Some days later the neighbor who Jane told me about called. We instantly start to talk like old friends just catching up, and Jennifer says it was great I was considering going to Houston. Finally, to my greatest surprise she brought up John of God.

Filled with surprise, I say, "Really? You have heard of him? I'm from Brazil and I never heard of him until very recently." She told me she had seen someone in California, a healer, who had been an apprentice at "The Casa" ("The Home," as the location where John of God sees people is called). She added that she didn't care what anyone thought, that she did it for her own spiritual healing. What a surprise to hear that!

Now I am starting to get curious about this John of God. Even my neighbor knows about him, and I, a Brazilian, never heard of him. Hum! But, again, I didn't look him up.

June 14, 2013 – Friends

Just as my neighbor Jane predicted, some friends have gotten closer, giving me their much-appreciated full support. Robina, Joy, Gideon and Martha are near and they have been instrumental in helping me cope. I feel eternal gratitude towards them, deep in my heart. At the same time, a few haven't even contacted me, falling off the radar, and a couple of others have retreated, avoiding much contact with me. I feel their distance, and it hurts that my diagnosis is uncomfortable to them. Cancer isn't contagious! Another tough new lesson learned: Cancer causes loss of friends. A couple of friends invited us to have lunch out. We go to a Caribbean restaurant. A guy who was introduced to me many months ago, and I haven't seen since, was also invited. I realize he doesn't know about my diagnosis, and I don't go into it. Today, I don't feel like spreading the cancer news.

June 20-22, 2013 – Visiting a Very Special Family in South Carolina

I felt an urge to go visit Maya and her adoptive parents in South Carolina.

Who is Maya? A girl I met at the orphanage I helped at in Nepal, back in April 2010. I posted the story of the orphanage on my travel blog, including her picture at the beginning of the entry. Four months later, I arrive in Greece, and receive a message from a couple in South Carolina, asking if I knew the name of the girl on the picture featured on my blog. Their message also told me the U.S. had frozen all adoptions from Nepal, five days after they were matched to a girl they believe is the one I met and posted pictures of on my travel blog. I confirmed that yes the girl was indeed Savalta. They asked if I could help them, as they were considering going to Nepal and hiring a lawyer to be able to adopt their child. And so I did, writing a letter to be used by the lawyer in the adoption process and allowing my blog to be used as evidence that the child was indeed an orphan. Fast forward, and on February 23, 2011, Maya arrives in the USA as a citizen, being held by her loving parents. I sent them early photos and videos of their daughter…. So surreal that I met her and bonded with her before they did and I could share footages of her.

Her parents and I communicated through messages, making a promise that we should meet soon, but life got busy. Now, a couple of years later, I want to see her and meet her parents, so I head to Venice, South Carolina.

Amazingly, I find myself at Maya's home, seeing her again after 3 years and meeting her parents for the first time. She has grown so much and doesn't look like the shy girl covered in prickly rash I met at the orphanage. She has an outgoing personality, and we bond instantly. The same thing happens with her parents. It feel like I had known them for the longest time. Her mom tells me everyone told her to give up on the adoption except for me and I helped her to move forward with the process. Wow! I wasn't aware of that. Her father is a physician, and he was incredible at giving me hope for the future, encouraging me to see the cancer as a chronic condition I had to learn to live with, just as I taught my patients to live with diabetes. It was difficult to see my condition from this perspective, but that was a new concept I could use on my quest to find "positivity" within my freaking diagnosis.

The amazing moments of happiness we spent together almost made me forget about the darn dragon, and that felt good.

By the way, another child, a little boy who called me Missy-Missy, was also featured on my blog, and the prospective parents also used it during his adoption process. He now lives with a loving family in California. Ah, the joys of "coincidences!"

June 23, 2013 – More Encouragement to Search for John of God and Finding Dr. Weiss (Who Later Tells me, "There are No Coincidences")

As I returned home, my friend from California had sent another message about John of God and also left voicemails. So, I finally decided to look into it, so I wouldn't be rude to her.

As I typed *John of God* on Google, Dr. Brian Weiss pops up on the screen as one of the links. I recognize his name as I had read his book "*Many Lives, Many Masters*" 8 years before and I am instantly drawn to the blue color of the cover and the title of his latest book "*Miracles Happen*."

Leaving my search for John of God aside, I go on to look Dr. Weiss up. Ah! One can meet him on workshops, retreats, and even cruises. Interesting!

The next day I find a free 36-minute past life regression video of his on YouTube. I knew I wanted to check it out, out of curiosity, but I didn't. Instead, I buy and start reading the book "*Miracles Happen*." I get intrigued. I want a miracle of my own; I want the dragon to go away forever.

"Vision is the art of seeing the invisible." — Jonathan Swif

GOING TO MD ANDERSON CANCER CENTER

I decided to make an appointment at MD Anderson, the biggest cancer center in the world. I didn't expect that anything new would be reviewed, but I wanted to be in their database, just in case I needed further options in the future. Besides, I had already met my high insurance deductible. So, I flew with my husband to Houston to put my mind more at ease,... or so I thought.

June 26, 2013 - And "The Cats" Sneak into My Life

We arrived in Houston late afternoon, had dinner and settled to rest for the 7:30 a.m. appointment at the gynecology oncology clinic next morning. I remembered the link for Dr. Weiss's regression, put on my headphones, and searched for the link, without any expectations, and clueless about how and why this would be done. I was curious and actually more interested about whether this would have any link whatsoever to the miracles that (possibly) can happen. I clicked Start, and began with the visualization of the beautiful garden, as guided. Just a few minutes had passed when, all of a sudden, I see (in my mind), no background at all. The garden and all had disappeared. I "saw" just me, sitting on the gray concrete-like ground. The background was gray. There was no color, no objects, nothing but me. I turn my head to the right and down, and right by me, there is a gray cat lying down. I suddenly felt like my body detached, and it moved up in the air, very fast. My heart started to race, for real. I could feel it pounding. I looked down from above, up in the air, and I could see the gray cat, who started to slowly shrink, getting smaller, smaller, and smaller, until it disappeared. I opened my eyes, in panic, my heart still pounding fast, and I tell my husband. "What the heck? That was so scary! I was supposed to be relaxing but the freakiest thing just happened!" I went on to describe the event and added, "I'm not even fond of cats." It took a while but I eventually slept.

June 25, 2013 – At Third Sarcoma Center

At 7:30 a.m. I was at the gynecology clinic at MD Anderson.

The young doctor who saw me graduated from UF, the university in my town back in Florida. She reported that they found cancer cells also in the lymphatic way, not just in the fibroid. (The other centers said the cancer was fully contained, and now it is not?) She also said the chance of survival was 50 percent and that there was no way to predict who gets that chance. Also, the malignancy was of the highest grade: 3.

So, the news gotten were even worse than the 75 percent, then 57 percent survival rate, but somehow I took it okay! She also added that there was no point in sending me to the sarcoma center yet, and agreed with the plan to check up every three months for surveillance and surgery if it was to appear elsewhere. And of course, she added that what I could do was "to be positive".

My husband and I had lunch and decided to go for a walk. I tried to brush off the additional negative news, which came just as I had started to feel a little more positive. Remember, positivity was the only thing suggested to me, and I was trying to hold on to the only log I had, in order not to drown in the ocean of helplessness.

As I walk, a friend called, and when I said the news was a little worse, she snapped, "You are going to be fine, like our friend Kim's cat."

"What about Kim's cat?" I ask curiously.

"Kim's cat had a sarcoma and the vet said it only had some months to live. This was two and a half years ago, and the cat is alive and cancer free."

I laugh. "So interesting! Last night I was meditating and a cat appeared in my mind, I felt I got out of my body, and then the cat shrunk until it disappeared. It freaked me out but now I may be like

Kim's cat and survive. I like this cat better! I'll take it." I say joking. We laugh. I relax.

Back in the hotel I fell an impulse to check the dates of Dr. Weiss's workshop again. A three-day event was to happen in New York in three weeks. I ponder aloud about going.

My skeptic husband says, "Go!" to my great surprise.

My daughter says, "Go!" also to my surprise... and I consider going.

All fired up to tame The Dragon by the Volcano Arenal in Costa
Rica.

*"The brave man is not he who does not feel
afraid, but he who conquers that fear."*
— Nelson Mandela

FAMILY TRIP TO CENTRAL AMERICA
AND PRACTICING COURAGE

In a melodramatic moment, while tears roll down, I tell my kids that I really want to take a family trip since it might be our last one. Amanda protested, saying I better not think this way. I said she was right, but it was just hard to think into the future now.

Within two days we booked a trip to Nicaragua and Costa Rica. I also decided to book the trip to Omega Institute in New York, to see Dr. Brian Weiss and discover what the "Miracles Happen" was all about.

As we are rushing out the door on the way to the airport, I vent: "Darn it! I forgot to get a book to read." Amanda tells me to hold on, as she just borrowed a book she thinks I might enjoy. It was *"The Book of Secrets"* by Dr. Deepak Chopra. She was right; I couldn't put it down. I am introduced to new concepts regarding how I can gain some control over my life and my health, which at the moment seemed out of my grasp. A new phase begins for me, on this journey with The Dragon. It might even start looking as an ally, not the enemy, somehow!

Nicaragua is blissful and quiet. There is reading time on a hammock, walks, driving through small villages, and volcano views. But my adventurous spirit woke up one day, and I suggested that we go Canopy Zip-Lining. Scared? Absolutely! But I find myself ready to practice courage. If I'm to learn to be brave to slay "The Dragon" (LMS), I shouldn't be scared of hanging from a cable on top of tall trees, right? And so I go, heart pounding at first, but determined to find courage and have fun along the way. And so it was.

Costa Rica isn't as relaxing as Nicaragua, as a tourist trap atmosphere has set in around Volcano Arenal, where we are staying. But making the most of each day is my mission, and besides hiking, I decide to practice a little more courage, this time rappelling on waterfalls. Yap! With fear and all, I find myself jumping backwards and down from high platforms, not knowing what was below, where my feet would land. Just like what might lie ahead for me... uncertainty. But, at the end of yet another day, I felt a sense of accomplishment and had had lots of fun with my daughter Amanda, who is a trooper. What else could I wish for this very day? To be cured, having The Dragon flee from my body forever.

Puzzled that I haven't received confirmation from Omega, although I gave a credit card number and all, I send them an email. The reply says that I was not registered! I write in panic, saying that I booked with a non-refundable ticket, hotel, and rental car, and that I must be registered. I get a confirmation that I am in! Wow! What a relief! (Later I find out that 12 days in advance, tickets are sold-out. It is a miracle that I got in? Hmm!)

"There are only two ways to live your life. One is as though nothing is a miracle. The other is as if everything is." — Albert Einstein

MIRACLE HAPPENS WORKSHOP AND TOO MANY "COINCIDENCES" TO BE IGNORED

Within 10 days I flew from home in Gainesville to Nicaragua and Costa Rica with the family, and then on my own to upstate New York to participate on the workshop Miracle Happens.

The accounts I will share next may seem "unique", to put it lightly, and I have no specific expectations on how readers will react to them. If you chose to believe in them or not, it is up to you. Just know that the events were lived by me and they have shaped my life in unexpected ways.

July 12, 2013 – Omega Institute with Dr. Weiss and Doing "Regression!"

I landed in New York, got the rental car and drove north for 5 hours, arriving only 30 minutes before Dr. Weiss got on stage, since I encountered traffic jams and also got lost. Exhausted, with a massive migraine, I sat on the floor of the room packed with 500 people. Not only was it a little overwhelming, but also I found myself disappointed.

"I am here to learn to relax and view death differently," I thought. *"How in the hell am I going to accomplish this in this huge room, with this many people?"* My only option as an answer was simple. *"Whatever... I'm here, so I may as well go with the flow. Accept what I can't change."*

That night, Dr. Weiss guided the group into a regression into the womb, before birth, and the time of birth. Beforehand, he advised that 40% of the group would not be able to successfully regress, and that these people should just accept it. To my greatest surprise, despite the migraine, I was able to do it. Tears rolled down my face, as I understood the reason why I was born. It all made sense in a fraction of a second. The rejections, and so much more... hard to share the stuff that involves years and years of my life.

I finally could accept the void I felt as a child, the lack of parental affection. I realized I wasn't born to be my parents' child. I was born to be Preta's daughter, the nanny who loved me unconditionally, who made me feel protected. She became my godmother, even though it was unheard of that a maid would become a godmother in Brazil. Preta passed away 15 years ago but I still think of her as my angel, and I now know why.

During the same regression, although Dr. Weiss didn't guide us to do anything else, I saw myself by her deathbed. I felt she knew I was there, at least in spirit. I always felt guilty that I was not there when she died. By that time, I already lived in the USA.

Dr. Weiss brought us back to the present day. I was astonished! So intense, surreal, but I had a sense of peace. Walking to the car, at 10:30 p.m., I exchanged words with a couple. They went to school in the city I currently live in. I keep finding people from Gainesville at the oddest places! It was 11:15 p.m. when I arrived at the hotel. Despite being very tired, I couldn't sleep and wouldn't until much later.

July 13, 2013 - Day 2 at Omega: "The Cat" Re-Appears and Dr. Weiss Talks to Me!

At 7:30 a.m. I decide to eat breakfast. Not much sleep, but I feel refreshed somehow. I wander around the beautiful setting — gardens, trees, Buddha statues, bunnies, and birds. Peace fills the air. My eyes find a group of seven iron sculptures.

"Oh my God!" I thought. *"That's the exact shape, or shadow, or silhouette, I saw coming out of my tummy in a dream the night when my 8-month baby died inside of me!"* I approach the artwork. A plaque says something that doesn't make any sense to me. I take

pictures and head to the auditorium, thinking of the night when I lost my son.

This time I sit in the fourth row of chairs, directly across from where Dr. Weiss will sit later. I didn't know where he would sit at the time. He comes in, chats and reminds everyone he will not answer personal questions since there's no time and the answers are probably on his YouTube channel. He also reminds us to respect his break time. It's the biggest group ever.

He guides us through another regression. This time it's a childhood memory. I find myself back at the sugar cane plantation in Northeast Brazil, where I lived until age seven.

I suddenly recall (or maybe relive) a nightmare I had when I was 4 or 5 years of age. I'm outside, not that far from the home. I'm alone. I feel the dirt under my feet. It's daytime, but when I look up I see three moons. One or two of them has a yellow tint. The ground starts to move in a wave-like motion. I look at the tall chimney of the sugar mill and it starts to crumble down. I'm frightened. I have remembered this dream from time to time over the past 45 years. Why, I don't know.

Next, Dr. Weiss tells the group that each person should find a partner, someone we don't know. Like I know anyone here anyway, I thought. My eyes meet those of a young guy, around 23 years old. He's in the very first row, towards the left of the stage. We both nod, and I walk towards his seat. We introduce ourselves.

"Mark, from Canada," he says.

"Patricia, from Florida," I say.

Dr. Weiss interrupts. "Don't exchange any further information. Just exchange an object with each other that can fit in your hands. Anything. A ring, keychain, et cetera."

I give Mark my earring, with the Buddhist symbol of the eternal knot. I figure if he has to say anything about me, he'll guess I have been to Tibet or I like Buddhism. He looks helpless searching himself for an object — no watch, no ring, no chain, and no small object at all.

"Ah!" He says, as he reaches for the aluminum water bottle by his side, unscrewing the top and giving it to me.

All I can think is that "I'm about to make a fool of myself if Dr. Weiss wants us to guess things by holding this stuff."

And so he says, "We are going to do an exercise called telemetry. Close your eyes as you hold the object in your hands."

I don't remember exactly what he said after, but he guided us to see scenes.

Immediately I visualize the young man on a bike heading South and West, and as the visions continue, I think, *"Darn it! This is about me, not him. Bike, going to Southeast Asia, Bali. What a fool I am!"*

We are told to open our eyes and share with each other what we saw in our minds. I ask to go first, so I could quickly get over my embarrassment of saying things pertaining to myself, and not Mark.

"I saw you on a bike," I say.

"I ride a bike all the time," he says.

"You're heading southwest, far away," I add. "Then you were in Southeast Asia."

He says, smiling as if astounded, "I live in Southeast Asia — in Singapore!"

How lucky I feel. I guessed two things right. Hoorah for me!

Then I add, "But I saw you in Bali, not in Singapore."

"I have been to Bali," he adds as he smiles. "I actually bought this water bottle there."

No way! I freak. I'm flabbergasted, as well as puzzled. I got goose bumps. He's surprised. I continue to say I saw a different scene as well, a clay pot with some coins and paper, maybe money, inside. There was also a long big knife, on a leather case, behind it on a rustic wooden shelf.

"What kind of knife?"

"Like the one I saw a man making on a hill tribe on North Myanmar."

He is interested, but confused as well. He shares that he has been planning to go to Myanmar, and I say jokingly, "Maybe you will see the knife there." Now it's his turn to tell me what he saw.

He hesitantly says, "Well! All I saw was a cat, just a cat and nothing else."

"What? A cat? What about this cat?" I franticly ask, with butterflies in my stomach. "What the heck?" I say to myself, puzzled.

"It was just there, walking. It looked happy. Yes, a happy cat."

Now I'm very intrigued. "What color was the cat?"

He closes his eyes, as if looking for the answer, and says, "Yellow." In a flash of a second, I'm relieved it's not the same gray cat I've seen, but still with his eyes closed, he says, "No, wait. It wasn't yellow. It was actually a gray cat."

Oh my God! My mind begins to spin, traveling back to Houston, my freaky vision during relaxation. Kim's cat. I'm spooked and shaky.

"Did you see anything else?" I ask.

"After the cat I just saw a scene of a family eating around a table. Everyone was happy. That's it."

My heart is pounding hard as Dr. Weiss announces it's time for a break. I impulsively get up, turn around, and find myself in front of him on the stage. I burst out, "Do you want to hear about my cats?" I mean, what kind of question is that? To Dr. Weiss of all people? The famous Dr. Weiss who already asked not to be approached during breaks.

"Yes," he says. "After I return from the bathroom." I can't believe what I just asked and that he consented to answer.

My mind is in a heavy fog. I push my way toward two women who had shared earlier that they have lots of the number 23 between them. I tell them I have a collection of 23s myself, 11 of them as a matter of fact. (I'll share that later, though.)

As I turn to go back to my seat, Dr. Weiss steps back on the stage. I walk towards him and ask, "Can I tell you now about my cats?"

"Yes!" He smiles.

"About three months ago I was diagnosed with cancer. About three weeks ago I was in Houston for another opinion and I was listening to your YouTube regression when I saw a gray cat by me. Then I felt like I was suddenly out of my body. My heart pounded, and it was scary. The next day I get a little worse news about the cancer, but my friend said I 'was going to be like a friend's cat.' That cat had cancer like mine but is still alive and cancer free after two and a half years. And now during the telemetry exercise Mark says all he saw was a cat. A gray cat! Isn't that weird? Freaky? Spooky?"

Instead of answering my questions, Dr. Weiss asks one of his own. "How did you do on the telemetry exercise?"

"Weird. I guessed everything right somehow. Do you want to sit?" What nerve I have, right? Asking Dr. Weiss to sit!

But he says yes and sits in his chair. I kneel on the floor in front of him.

He looks into my eyes with two fingers pointing at them and says: "You can go very deep (new vocabulary to me). I can see it. Your eyes roll back very far." (I didn't know I was rolling my eyes back.) Now the blow: "You can heal yourself. Go see John of God."

I felt the blood leave my face. I look down. I feel a tear run down my left cheek. "No! You don't understand. I was Googling John of God when I found you on the computer screen. I am thinking of going on your cruise at the end of the month."

"No. You did the work here already. Go see John of God in Brazil."

"I'm from Brazil." He says, "Better." With my mind spinning, I continue, with trembling lips. "I didn't come here because of the cancer. I told my family I came here to see death differently and to learn to relax/meditate more, but deep inside, I was also puzzled by my many coincidences, which happen all over the world. I mean, the kids I find to help heal, the dreams of death I have before it happens." I'm trembling all over as I speak.

I don't remember Dr. Weiss's exact words from this point on, but he said something about "accepting it" and that I could "synchronize" and do "channeling" of some sort. These are all new words and concepts for me.

I kept on insisting on an explanation about how Mark saw just the gray cat. One thing I am absolutely sure that Dr. Weiss firmly said is "There are no coincidences. Forget the cats. Go see John of God."

Dr. Weiss did not suggest that I go; he basically told me to go. I thanked him. At least I think I did and went back to my seat, shaking. I don't know how long we talked, but it seemed a long time. It was all too surreal. Was this a miracle happening?

For the rest of the day Dr. Weiss would tell the audience about the ability to roll the eyes way back, which is associated with the ability to "go deep," to hypnotize easily. He also said something about those who have the ability to connect to others in indiscernible ways, to predict events, and that those people shouldn't be afraid and should turn off their left brain. You know, the analyzing part of the brain — the part that tries to justify everything with concrete facts.

"He is talking about you, isn't he?" asked the woman next to me. With a helpless gaze, I nodded and said, "I think so."

The next portion of the workshop involved a healing regression (or exercise). I got comfortable, lying down on the floor. I concentrated on the cancer I was diagnosed with two months before. I had meditated on it previously, visualizing the mass as red. It made sense since I had been a medical student years ago and could picture how it would look. But now, suddenly, my vision changed. The mass was black, and inside of it there was an embryo, also black. The whole picture was black. Surprisingly, that grim picture didn't frighten me, but as I was brought back, I couldn't shake the feeling that it was somehow connected to the first regression the night before, the one before birth.

I raised my hand to share the experience, but I wasn't selected. I still don't know what that could mean. I don't think it was the son I lost in uterus.

Dr. Weiss chose three people to share their regressions, including a woman seated way in the back of the room. I couldn't see her, and all I could hear was her repeating several times, "the dragon." That is the nickname for my type of sarcoma. The Leiomyosarcoma Foundation slogan is, "Together we can slay the dragon."

When the session was over and people were leaving, I walked to the back of the room. "Excuse me," I asked a woman. "Do you know who was talking about the dragon?"

She pointed to an empty row of seats. "Oh. It was a woman sitting over there. But she has left already." I thanked her, and turned to exit.

"Are you the person looking for the woman with the dragon?" A woman startled me, walking in from outside. I answered "yes."

"That was I. I don't have much time, maybe a couple of minutes. What do you want to know?"

Well, we talked for almost an hour. She told me I didn't want to slay the dragon. "You need to love it," she said. "You also need to learn to love yourself."

She was direct, firm, and loving at the same time. She comforted me, and I took a "figa," a Brazilian good luck charm, from my necklace and handed it to her.

"No, honey. Don't give it to me. That belongs to you. Can I make a prayer with it first?" After, she opens her eyes and handed it back to me. She also said something about the fact that it was no accident I ended up on the stage talking privately with Dr. Weiss, pointing out how I looked, kneeling in front of him.

I had lunch alone but a couple of women came and went, sharing my table. Still "spooked" by the morning happenings, I also felt joyful... Hard to explain. I walked out through a beautiful path bordered by yellow day lilies. I asked a young woman to take a picture of me walking away. "Just my back," I said.

When I looked over my pictures later, she had taken a photo of me walking forward as well. I looked carefree and even smiled! I love that shot. It brings back all of the intensity of my first 8 hours at Omega, in a light, cheerful way.

The afternoon session began and this time the regression was to a past life. Again, I thought, "Here I go. Whatever... dream, imagination, reality, whatever it is, without judging, just like Dr. Weiss reminds us." He repeated many times, "Just try not to judge, critique. Let it be."

Eyes closed, I hear his instructions to visualize doors, each from a different time. We are to choose one of them. The years are 1800s, 1500s, 1300s....

"Oh, come on," I think. "Go further down, further, further down in time."

I start to get frustrated, afraid he won't name a time for me to enter that particular door.

"This last door you can open to go even further down in time," he finally says. Immediately, I open the door and look down at my feet. No shoes. Small woman's feet — dirty, very dirty. Then I realize I am the woman with undone dry hair, brownish skin, with pieces of animal skin covering my body, like a robe.

I am in a cave, clutching a baby: my baby. There are three men in front of me talking to each other. They are deciding the fate of my deformed baby. Nobody knows who the father is. I feel like it is the ways of the tribe. The women slept with many men, as they wished. My deformed baby is considered a curse, or something like that. The men are deciding how to get rid of him. The younger man seems to disagree with the other two. He sees that I am listening to the conversation, but doesn't announce it.

Next, I am running, holding my baby very tight, with the wind blowing behind me. My dirty, messy hair blows on the side of my face as I run through arid terrain, for a long, long time.

Then time moves forward. I'm near a waterfall. I spend a while there, years maybe. I bathe my son. I scrub him.

Time lurches forward again, some 15 years later. I am around a fire. It's nighttime. There's a group of people from another tribe. I am smiling, talking. Happy. I look across the fire on the ground and see my son — probably 15 years old now. He's happy too. I realize I've never had another man, content being a mother with a group of people who accept us. We are part of their family, their tribe.

As Dr. Weiss brought us back, I thought of Komang, the Balinese boy with an extremely rare skin disorder. I found him a year ago. At age three and a half he had never received treatment. He lived in pain with deformed face, hands, and feet. I suddenly had the impression that he was my son in the cave time. Weird, I know. My imagination went wild…. All I know is that I felt peace.

So, over dinner that night I find myself saying to people, "Do you want to meet my son?" I share pictures taken 13 months ago, when I hiked up to Komang's little home on the top of a hill in Northern Bali. I tell them how he's now walking, talking, relieved and healthier, after I brought the diagnosis and treatment he needed. He is even happy. I also thought of my 17-year-old son from my current life. Why? I have no clue.

I remember crossing the door and looking at my feet at yet another regression. I was a man, a big man. My feet are dusty, and I am wearing sandals. Leather, not factory made, handmade, and rustic. My clothes are rustic too. I carry a weapon, and I'm alone.

I see the west hills and green ahead of me. I'm walking home. I've been walking for a long time and will walk for a while longer. I see the rustic little home up ahead, almost at the edge of a soft rolling hill. I see the smoke reaching the sky. My wife is cooking. I open the door. The kids—three I think—two boys and a girl. They happily hug me. They're ages 3 to 7 or so. I stand up and glance at my wife, who smiles. Her hair is in a bun, pulled back covering her ears. We don't hug. We just smile at each other. There was love, serenity, and that's all I needed.

Somehow, I feel like I am her too! I feel like her now, but also felt like him, particularly before he entered the home.

Dr. Weiss told us to go further, to the end of that life. I'm lying on a small bed. I'm her, the mother. I'm at peace. I have a high fever. I lay straight, hands crossed at chest level. The kids are just a little older: young teens. My husband is there too. I'm at peace, and I counsel them to be in peace as well. Soft tears gently roll down our faces. I die.

Bizarre? Surreal? Yes, absolutely! However, it is all so magical at the same time.

July 14, 2013: Guided to Go Further in Time and Going Back Home

It's the last day of my time with Dr. Weiss. He announces we will visit a future life. He puts us all mentally in an elevator of some sort. He gives us instructions slowly, but I want to go fast. I can't wait to get off. Well, when I step out, I find myself in space, as blue energy. No arms, or legs or face. It's a long, thin shape, royal blue and some lighter shades of blue. The energy slowly circulates. I am this energy form, floating in space. I can't see anything else. All I know is that I am far from our Earth world. I feel peaceful, just there with energy softly moving inside my "body."

I leave Omega filled with joy, happiness! I drive to New York in peace. During my flight to Orlando, I put my headphones on and realize I am singing. After landing, I feel like skipping, not walking. I am as light as a happy child. I drive home joyfully.

I arrive at 10:00 p.m., and my son tells me my doctor left many messages. It didn't worry me. The next day I check the message, which says they found a lesion on my left breast on the CT-scan and the doctors recommend a mammogram and ultrasound of the breast ASAP. I am puzzled but not concerned. Two days later I have the ultrasound and repeat the mammogram. I am in a tiny room waiting for the results for a very long time. A nurse comes in and says the mammogram needs to be repeated. Now I find myself a little worried. After the mammogram, the doctor comes in and says it was just a benign cyst, and actually the second image showed it smaller.

And so I had the first false alarm and unnecessary stress.

*"You travel to search and you come back home to find
yourself there."* — Chimamanda N Adichie

SEARCHING FOR AND FINDING JOHN OF GOD

As soon as I arrive back home, I start my online search,
investigating "John of God" and becoming more and more surprised
that I've never heard about him before. He's been on television over
a few years now: Primetime, CNN, Dr. Oz, and Oprah more than
once. *Where had I been?*

I text Thania, a Brazilian who lives in California and takes
groups to see John of God a couple times per year. I needed to know
a little more before I considered travelling to Brazil. She calls me and
shares a short version of her story. She hurt her spinal cord badly
in an accident. She had the feeling of pinpricks all over and had
difficulties and pain. She went to John of God and ended up staying
3 months, then a year. That's when John of God told her she would
go to another country and marry a "specific man."

She has completely healed (having X-rays to prove it), moved
to the USA, and has been married to an American for 5 years. She
conducts healing, and meets with groups of people. She doesn't
charge.

She asked me about Dr. Weiss and mentioned it was her dream
to meet him. I shared the briefest version of my story, starting with
the experience in Houston, with the gray cat, the telemetry with the
guy seeing just a gray cat, and Dr. Weiss telling me "You can go very
deep, you can heal yourself. Go see John of God."

She said she got goose bumps when I spoke and that I should go
to Abadiânia soon.

"One or two weeks stay?" I asked.

"Buy an open-ended ticket," she answered.

I told her I'd wait for the next CT scan in a week before I made plans, but I couldn't go for more than 2, maybe 4 weeks. She goes on to say, "It's just what I see. You stay there for at least one month, but ultimately, the entities are who decide." Hmm!

July 21, 2013 – Getting More Unexpected Encouragement to Go See John of God

I go to the Tibetan Meditation Center where I practice and feel an urge to share the story with the resident lama, Lama Losang/ David Bole.

"Can I tell you the story about my cats?" I asked.

He smiles and says, "Of course." We discuss the auspiciousness of the day on the Tibetan calendar, how some crickets from a pet shop were released, and the fact that it is also Lama David's birthday.

"Do you know who Dr. Brian Weiss is?" I blurt out.

"Of course." He answers.

"Do you know who John of God is?" I ask.

"Of course." He answers.

I describe what has happened during the last 3 weeks.

"So, when are you going?"

"Do you think I should go?"

"Of course!"

"Well," I say, "I have the CT scan tomorrow and the results in three days. I'll wait, and if the results are good, I'll make arrangements."

"Why? You should go either way, even if, or particularly if, the results are negative. There are no coincidences. It was all lined up for you. I'd go. Go, and share when you get back."

Wow! What a surprise! I left and looked into the ticket to Brazil.

"Serendipity, the art of making happy discoveries." — Unknown

NO SIGNS OF THE DRAGON AND MY COLLECTION OF NUMBER 23

I handled the CT very well — no fainting this time. On July 23, I got an email from my oncologist, the day before our appointment. "All good. No sign of cancer." Yes! Yes! Pure relief. I feel happiness, joy, and bliss. Now I can "go." I went on to get my ticket and 7 days later I arrived in Abadiânia, Brazil.

So, here I am, introducing to you my interesting "collection of the number 23:"

January 23, 2014	News of LMS metastasis
February 23, 2011	Orphaned Nepalese girl arrived in The United States
April 23, 2013	Diagnosis of Leiomyosarcoma
July 23, 2013	CT scan news shows no metastasis
July 23, 1992	Birthday of two twin nephews
August 23, 2012	Birthday of puppy I adopted
August 23, 1981	Birthday of another nephew
August 23, 2013	I leave Abadiânia
September 23, 1990	Birthday of my daughter
September 23, 2013	I discover the cat drawing on the box of my son's ashes

October 23, 1995	Birthday of my son
November 23, 1958	Birthday of my sister
November 23	Birthday of friend who helps me with ill kids in Bali
November 23, 2013	Moosewood becomes a special sanctuary to me

At Omega, I met 2 women with many 23s also. They became my friends.

At the Casa Dom Ignacio, just as I arrive, a group is gathering to sing songs from a book with 55 pages. The first song called was on "Page 23: Alleluia."

I am not suggesting that there is any specific meaning to all these 23s. I just find it a little odd and definitely interesting, so, I shared.

July 29, 2013 – Introduction to *Spiritism*

Growing up in Brazil, I was aware of the doctrine of spiritism. Spiritism is the belief in the survival of the human spirit/soul after death and reincarnation. It also often includes the practice of trying to make contact with the spirits of people who have died. At least in Brazil, this is often done at *Spirit Centers,* by mediums. A person who is adept of Spiritism is called a *spiritist*. A French, Allan Kardec, who wrote several books about mediumship and contacting the dead, including The Book of the Spirits, initiated the diffusion of Spiritism.

There are different types of mediums, those who have contact with the spirit of those who have passed away. John of God, or medium João, as he prefers to be called, is considered an incorporated medium. He says to get *incorporated* by the spirit of several deceased doctors, and under that state, act as a doctor able to treat, cure, or improve the health of thousands of people. He has been doing this work for 59 years, never charging for the service he provides. For a couple of decades, he has been seeing thousands of people, from all over the world, at the Casa Don Ignacio de Loyola, three days per week. Again, the doors are open to all, and the medium does not charge for his service.

"Once the soul awakens, the search begins and you can never go back." —John O'Donohue

AND TO BRAZIL I GO TO MEET THE HEALER JOHN OF GOD

July 30, 2013 - Arrival in Abadiânia to Meet John of God and More Cats Appear

The taxi driver picks me up at the hotel in Brasilia, and I ask to stop at the Cathedral, before moving on to Abadiânia. I love the colors of the stained glass artwork on the ceiling and walls; my colors: blue and light green. The angels hanging from the ceiling/sky are divine. I say a prayer and go.

Arriving at the Dom Ingrid Inn, the driver, Amos, talks to a young woman at the reception desk and takes me to my room. He drops my blue bag by the door of room 52. I pay him, close the door behind me, and turn around. There, on the wall, above my bed, is a colorful picture.

"Nooo! No way! Cats!" I say out loud.

There are seven of them on this tacky picture. I turn around and leave the room, to find the ladies who clean the rooms.

"Hi. I was just wondering. Do most of the rooms have pictures of animals on the walls?" I ask the young woman caring cleaning supplies.

"There are no pictures in the rooms, I don't think," the woman says, looking confused.

"Okay, thanks," I say, walking away.

I head back to the room, now puzzled.

Over lunch, I ask the reception girl, "Do you know who chose my room?"

"What do you mean?" she asks.

"I was just wondering if all the rooms have pictures on the wall, like, you know, of little animals." She frowns. "I really don't know what you mean."

I realize it's time to let go of the cats, but I can't help but wonder if Ricardo, the guide I exchanged two emails with about my room reservation, didn't know something about *the cats*, although I didn't mention anything.

Four days later I asked him if he picked my room. "No, they are assigned as people check in. Why?"

That's when I said, "I may tell you later, someday. Maybe it's just a coincidence."

"There are no coincidences," he says. And I smile, walking away.

Back to the first day: After lunch, I walk to the Casa de Dom Ignacio and wander around the grounds. The wooden benches under the mango trees are inviting. I sit down and contemplate the vast view of the mountains and valley. The birds chirp, and I marvel in serenity. The sky is blue, not a cloud above. It is cool, refreshing, and I am here. I'm present, but still unsure why, and puzzled by the chain of events of the past few weeks, which brought me to this place, this moment. I remind myself, "Let it be." I turn around to see a group of people gathering around some tables across the garden. I approach, sit down, and see that they are about to start singing. A woman with long dark hair and the most beautiful blue eyes announces that anyone can call songs by the pages of the books being passed around. I hear out loud a person saying, "Number 23." "Ah, 23!" Hmm. All start to sing "Alleluia," I smile, and I sing along.

After a delicious buffet dinner at the inn, I join a group of people at the Casa for a group prayer. Walking out after it's finished, I tell a man, "Beautiful family you have!"

I had noticed his teenage daughter and small son. They had sat by me during the afternoon sing-along. He shares he's a physician who is here for the sixth time in 14 months. His wife, also a doctor, didn't come this time. She's back in Canada.

"What brought you here?" he asks me.

I shrug. "Not sure, exactly. I guess a series of coincidences. I bought my ticket just five days ago."

*"When you walk to the edge of all the light you have
and take that first step into the darkness of the unknown,
you must believe that one of two things will happen.
There will be something solid for you to stand upon or
you will be taught to fly."* — Patrick Overton

INTRODUCTION TO THE CASA & JOHN OF GOD

The first day at the Casa with João de Deus (John of God) and
I'm dressed all in white like everyone else. It's 7:30 a.m. and I'm
walking to the Casa with two people, one from California, where
I lived for 13 years, and one from Houston, where I was exactly a
month ago. There are so many people in white walking towards the
Casa, and even more already on its grounds. The gates are open and
anyone can walk in, one to two thousand people each Wednesday,
Thursday and Friday, even on holidays, without any charge.

I headed to my 20-minute "crystal bed" session even though I
didn't know what exactly it was, or did. It had been recommended
to me, so I took a chance. I was taken to a small room with a small
bed. On top of it rang flashing colorful crystals, which were pointed
to specific parts of my body. I just lay there, relaxing. (Much later I
find out the crystals colors and positions correspond to the chakra
points in the body. But even then, I didn't know what chakras were!)
Within minutes I worried that I'd be late to meet with Ricardo, the
guide. If I miss him, I don't know what to do or where to go. So
nothing special happens.

Afterward, I stand outside for a long time. Ricardo was late — in
the Brazilian, fashionable way. So many people arrive, all in white
clothing. A woman asks me if I am in line for translation. When I

answer no, I see the big gray cat face painted on her bag. Another cat? Really? I smile.

I ask a couple of people if they know Ricardo. One is from Houston, where I was a month ago and saw the first cat vision, and the other one from New York where I was 2 weeks ago and the reason I'm here. I keep getting goose bumps all the time.

Ricardo arrives and says, "I'll be inside by João de Deus, and you nod when you get close, on the line. Okay?"

But I have a couple of requests. I want him to talk for me, since I don't know what to say, and I want to ask first for a dear friend who is starting chemo this very day, for an unknown, inoperable tumor. "You speak Portuguese, so you talk." I insisted that I didn't know what to say, or even why I was here." He finally gave in and agreed to talk for me. About the second request, he said "It's not common that people ask for others on the first day, but since it's an emergency, and you are insistent, we can do it. Just give me his pictures."

I sit in the packed room. It's said to be a very auspicious day, the day that Saint Ignacio de Loyola's birth is celebrated and a week after João de Deus' birthday. I find myself saying a little prayer in Portuguese, Our Father. I had not said that prayer in a long time.

John of God suddenly shows up, unexpectedly, on stage and just smiles. I think he said a few words of thanks... Some people went through a door, what I now know leads to two meditation (current) rooms.

Lines are formed: one for people having surgery (spiritual ones) who are guided inside the "operation" room. People wanting physical surgery are also called to have "procedures"/surgeries done on stage.

I start to feel a little faint. With my history of passing out, I decide to ask some women if I could sit on the last bench in the room, behind them. Everyone is asked to stand, except for those who can't. I know I have to sit, or fall down. A woman asks me if I'm okay. I am, but I know I need to stay seated. Then a woman from the crowd outside walks in, and stands on the bench by me. "Stand up on the bench so you can see," she says to me. I look up, and it's the woman with the cat face bag!

"I don't know if I should," I say. She insists, and there I am standing on the bench. I could see John of God about to cut a man, to the right of his left nipple. I look away for a second. When I look back he wipes his bare hands with blood, with no gloves on! I sit down again. When my line is called I feel faint again. I keep breathing, deeply. Once inside, I realize people are all sitting in many lined up benches, with their eyes closed. There is a young guy guiding us in. He asks if I'm okay. I answer: "Yes, I am. I think so, but I'm a little dizzy."

"Just raise your hand if you need to. You'll be okay," he reassures me.

The line moves to the bigger "current" (meditation) room and I see John of God at the end of it. I see Ricardo. As I get closer I nod and give him the pictures I'm holding. Chester's three pictures. I don't remember seeing João de Deus's face at all! But I know I was in front of him. He scribbled something on a tiny piece of paper, an herbal supplement for my friend Chester to take for 40 days.

I do remember Ricardo saying I was there because I had surgery 3 months ago and had come to get rid of *the spider*. What spider? What an odd and confusing statement! What the heck?

After being guided to sit on a bench to get a "pass" (healing prayer by a medium), I walk out and find myself confused. What am I to do? Ricardo shows up, to my relief, and I ask what spider he was talking about.

"The *entities* don't use the word cancer. Cancer is physical, and it was already removed. The spider is what needs to be removed now, the source of the cancer, like stagnant feelings." Hmm. There I go again, not comprehending much, but choosing to go with the flow.

He adds the entity said for me to sit in the "current" (meditation) room in the afternoon and come back tomorrow for spiritual surgery the next morning.

Now I am getting that John of God is referred to as "Entity" when incorporated by a spirit. My new vocabulary is expanding!

I wrote for a while under the peaceful mango trees, and after lunch I was back in the main room and later standing in the current line. At 1:15p.m. I am sitting inside. A woman is giving instructions in English: "Keep your eyes closed during the whole current time, for however long it will take. The entity decides when it finishes. It can be 20 minutes to many hours. If you open your eyes, the current will be broken and the "work" of all others affected. If you are not able to sit for as long as it is needed, you need to leave now. If you need to go to the restroom, raise your hand, wait to be approached, go to the bathroom without talking to anybody, and come back directly to the current room, close your eyes, and continue your "work."

I closed my eyes, and surprisingly I could not turn the palms of my hands down, as I always kept during my meditation back home. (I always tried to keep my palms up, as Lama David says is preferred, but I never could do it, preferring my hands by my tummy). Now my hands are oddly, for me, facing up, and pretty quickly, my forearm is up in the air, elbows included. I think for an instant, "It's good that no one can see me since their eyes are closed too."

I smile and keep smiling. Soon after, a woman, who I now know as Heather, said, "It's good to keep a smile on your face." I felt at ease, and smiled even more, as I thought until then that it was weird that I couldn't wipe the smile off my face! The center of my palms start to feel hot and so they remained, only to feel much hotter when I could sense that people were walking in front of the room. At some point I felt that my right palm should face the right, and so I turned it. That's where the main room is. I had no clue what was going on, who was where, doing what. My eyes are closed. Then it was announced that Dom Ignacio de Loyola's spirit was incorporated into John of God. The announcer continues: "Dom Ignacio is here."

My hands got even hotter, very hot. At times my upper body swung back and forth. I was aware of it, knew it must look weird, but couldn't stop gently swinging! Much later, eyes still closed, tension on the shoulders coming and going, two fingers on each hand getting very hot, sometimes numb, on and off, I feel a strong and new feeling all over my body. It only lasted a second or so. I just go with the flow.

A man announces that the current is about to be over, to keep our eyes closed, but before ending, he says: the "Entity" has two messages for those on the current." First, he spoke for a long time and I didn't understand most of what he said, but I heard him repeating *falange*, a word I had never heard before. (Now I know it is a group of spirits working together). And then he said that the prayer current was very strong and the message was that everyone who was in this particular *current*, had their wishes granted." The whole message was in Portuguese, my native language, but I wasn't 100% sure I heard, or understood, it right. Besides, I didn't make a wish!

The second message was to drink the sacred water on the way out.

We could now open our eyes. I looked at my clock to find that 5 hours had passed! I could never meditate for more than a few minutes, unless it was chanting meditation, which I did in Tibetan, or guided by a tape. Wow! Five hours? I couldn't believe it. I walk out in a daze. Crossing the main hall, the woman with the cat bag, again, walked towards me and she asked if I was inside the current room. I said yes, and she asked if I understood what the first message was since it was in Portuguese. I said that I thought he said the wishes of all on the current were granted, but I wasn't really sure. She hugged me, thanked me, and I affirm again, that I wasn't sure if I understood it correctly and I'd prefer her to ask someone who really heard it well. She gazes around and points to the older man who I recognize from my inn, Sr. Noberto. The woman said he was the one who gave the messages.

Later I see the word written on a saying on a picture: *Falange*. But I still didn't understand what it meant. I walked out, and a few feet away I saw a man counting little plastic bags of shredded sweetened coconut with the vendor. I hear a woman passing by saying "That's João de Deus!" Hmmm! He is out here? No big crowd around him, counting coconut bags!

At an impulsive moment, I walk up to him and said, "Excuse me. Could I ask if you know who Dr. Brian Weiss is?" He just stared at me and handed me a coconut bag. I added, "the American doctor who wrote *Many Lives, Many Masters*. He continues to stare at me, without a word. I fell odd, kind of embarrassed, but I add, "Oh well! He knows who you are and encouraged me to come here. Thanks for the coconuts." (Later I find out that João de Deus is illiterate, he can't read or write. I felt so embarrassed I asked him about Dr. Weiss's book.)

"I'll be in the United States soon." he said as I turn to walk away.

I asked, "Omega?"

"Yes, Omega." he says.

I bought water and walked to my inn, kind of floating, smiling, and still amazed that I am actually in Abadiânia, a place I never heard of just a few days ago, and that I talked to and got coconut from John of God himself. Well... I am happy and that is great!

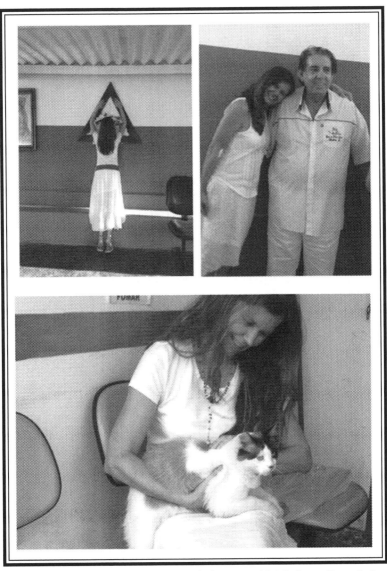

a) Saying a prayer at the triangle of The Casa. b) With medium João.
c) With "my" cat.

"There are two ways to be fooled. One is to believe what isn't true; the other is to refuse to believe what is true." — Soren Kierkegaard

MY SPIRITUAL SURGERY

There are hundreds of people in white already walking to the Casa at 7:00 a.m. and many more already there. I take a seat and wait. Eight people start praying the Hail Mary, and Our Father.

Like the day before, people line up for their surgeries. This time, so do I, and I feel well, not dizzy like the other day. We walk in and sit on benches. We are told to close our eyes. The "work/surgery" has started. The palms of my hands are hot. I was expecting perhaps a sensation in my stomach area, but I feel nothing. After a while I feel like a straw has been inserted on the top right side of my head, a couple of inches from my forehead. My forehead feels really strange. Then nothing. Soon after we're all told the "surgery" is complete and to walk outside and wait for instructions.

A man comes and instructs us to get a supplement at the pharmacy, have the free soup the casa offers, and go to bed (in our individual rooms) for 24 hours. We can have food delivered to the room, but we're to stay quiet. No talking, no cell phones, no reading, just rest.

I eat a bowl of soup and walk to my room. At 9:30 a.m. I feel no different. I nap off and on and worry I'll be up all night since I am not used to resting during the day. But no, I wake up a few times, but sleep quite well.

August 2, 2013 - The Day After the Spiritual Surgery

I wake, meditate, pray, practice some light yoga and eat breakfast. Then it's back to bed. I'm told I can't go back to the Casa until the afternoon.

When I return to the Casa later, I close my eyes. Again, I feel heat in the palms of both hands. Someone had told me to relax and concentrate. That's what I did. As people passed by me, the heat of my hands intensified. This time three of my fingers got so hot they were almost numb. This current lasted three and a half hours. When it's all done I feel happy, relaxed, well.

August 3, 2013 - It's Quiet in Abadiânia on "Non-Casa Days"

The rhythm of the small town is quieter. Many people have left since medium João de Deus is at the Casa only on Wednesday, Thursday, and Friday. Mostly foreigners remain. I have breakfast, and around 8:40 a.m. I go for a mile walk to the viewpoint. I meet a man from Europe. We exchange a few words.

"If you had surgery three days ago you are not supposed to be walking far or without an umbrella," he said.

"But it's only 9:00 a.m.," I tell him.

"The sun is strong. You shouldn't be walking without an umbrella."

Okay! Not very certain I need to, but I go back to my room. I read and listen to meditation apps. Later, I spend time on a hammock, just relaxing.

I decide to take a little walk in the afternoon to the Casa for the group prayer. I have borrowed an umbrella from my neighbors. I meet a woman from Houston at the bookstore and find myself asking about the meaning of certain crystals. I didn't know crystals had meaning, just until now that I hear her talking about them.

"You have a third eye that is opening," she says.

When I tell her I'm not sure what she meant, she says if I'm still confused about why I am here, I need to ask for clarity and release fear of my gift. Hmmm. Gift? (To this date Cree is still in touch with me.)

August 4, 2013 - Going to The Waterfall and Starting to Let Go of Resentment

I had asked when I could go to the *sacred waterfall* nearby and was told Sunday. After breakfast I read and meditate on healing. In the early afternoon I walk down the winding dirt road to the *"cachoeira"* (waterfall). It's warm. I have my neighbor's umbrella. As I walk, I think of a quarter century ago when I was pregnant with my first child.

I realize I have to let go of deep resentment, as writer Louise Hay would say. I dig deep down and suddenly feel resentment for the people I had told "I feel strange, and the baby is not moving." This happened when I was 8 months pregnant, back in 1988. At that time, I dreamt that a white light form (like a shape of a head and a body) left my tummy, from above the left pelvic bone.

The last person that I told the baby wasn't moving was a classmate from India. She had two daughters and reassured me, "That's normal. You are very big already. There isn't room for the baby to move."

Okay, she knows, I thought, so I figured I should let it go. She was wrong. *I was right.* In the middle of that night I woke up crying and saying, "Something is wrong! I can feel it." I went to get a pregnancy book and I found this passage: "If you feel no movement, for this many hours, call the doctor."

I sobbed. "See! I told everyone and they all told me to relax, that it was normal."

I called my doctor at 4:00 a.m. and was told, "Take a shower, lie in bed, and count the movements for an hour. Call me and go to the hospital if there are few movements."

I went to the shower, crying. I knew. Afterward, I lie in bed counting what I suspected were contractions, not movements. I called the doctor back, dressed, and headed to the hospital in Woodland, California, with my husband. By that time, it was getting light. There was a group of bikers on the road. I remember the sadness I felt, passing by the fields of nut trees. I knew something was very wrong. I just knew...

When the nurse did an ultrasound, she couldn't locate the heartbeat. I told her where to look, as I knew where the baby was, always. His hands I had "held" several times, his feet, I had "tickled," the head I had caressed.

She turned off the machine and started to head out of the room. When she got to the door, she turned to me, saying, "If you believe in God, start praying."

I sobbed. I am numb. I called my sister in Brazil. I felt helpless. We waited for the doctor. He walked in and said, "I'm sorry."

Now, I finally feel that all these years I have resented myself for not following my gut instinct. I knew something was wrong that day. I dreamed and I saw Bruno coming out of me. But I was young and had no experience, and I asked for answers. I had done my best, and I have to forgive myself, and besides, the baby's soul was already gone.

A week later I gave birth to my dead baby. I held his still body, and I had to say goodbye, just after I said hello.

Back to the present time, as I near the waterfall entrance, I see a covered area with some benches. A man and a woman are there.

"Are you from India?" I ask the woman as I approach her.

"Yes, I am. Are you alone without a guide?" I nod yes. "Why don't you wait for our guide as he'll explain about the waterfall?"

"Oh, okay. That would be nice. Thank you. I don't know anything about it."

She asks what has brought me here, and I tell the very short version, as the guide arrives. "You go in one at a time, women first," he says. "As you cross the first bridge alone, you stop, and let go of your past, the unresolved things. At the second bridge, you let go of the present, what brought you here. At the third bridge, right before the waterfall, you see what you want for your future."

He then tell us to hold hands, right palms up to give and left palms down to receive. The five of us make a circle, and a silent prayer. It feels peaceful. The birds sing, I can feel the prayers, and I am grounded on this very moment.

At the first bridge I let go of resentment for others and myself. At the second bridge I let go of what brought up the cancer, and ask to let go of fear of my "weird" ability to see events as I sleep, and at the third I asked for clarity about any ability I might have and to be free to accept the unknown. (Actually I didn't ask, I stated that I accept, I open up, and I surrender.)

The water is extremely cold, but I go under the small fall, feeling relief, like cleansing. I get out and in again, three times, receiving as I am under the cold water, and letting go as I move my body out. I feel great as I walk back past the third bridge and see a lizard on the path, right in front of me. That's the closest animal to a dragon around here, I thought. I extended both of my arms, shooing it away and saying, "Go!" It walks to the side. "Go!" and it walks some more. "Go!" and it disappears from my sight. I smile, and so goes my dragon (the nickname of Leiomyosarcoma, the type of cancer I have.)

August 5, 2013 – Frightening and Unexplained Pain

After breakfast, I head to the Casa for my 8:40 a.m. scheduled crystal bed session. As I wait, I notice the room assigned is the same as the session on July 31, when I felt nothing. I notice the small painting of a man's face. It's one I've seen many places around here, and suspect it is João de Deus as a young man. But no, a girl tells me, "That's Dr. Augusto." Ah! That's the entity, spirit, who performed my "spiritual surgery."

I get on the bed, cover my feet with a blue blanket, and relax without expectation. I close my eyes, and lay my palms up. The heat on my palms comes right away. My forehead feels "intense." I don't know how else to describe it. I feel pressure on my right ear, like on an airplane. Next, there is a strong sensation on my nose. These last for some minutes. As those sensations ease, I feel a sharp and short, pin-like pinch on the left side of my chest, about 3 inches below the collarbone. It's just for a second, so I don't freak out.

I relax, no sensations now, just the heat on my palms. All of a sudden I feel a tingle, like a current going up the right wall of my vagina, going up to where my uterus was before it was removed. It feels so strange. It won't go away. It's not painful at all, just a tingle, like static electricity. Hmm.... Interesting.

The session ends just as I feel my body change. It's different everywhere. I realize I have a smile on my face, despite the strangeness of it all. Oops! My womb area feels different. Gentle pain. It goes away.

I think of the kids in Asia, the ones I helped. I wonder why I'm thinking about them: Tibet, Nepal, Burma, Bali, and also Brazil.

People have often been intrigued about why and how I find them. I think, "Komang, I already knew him." I think of the regression in New York. "Maya, I think I knew her as well." I just let my mind wander, feeling love, and smiling.

I walk out and feel tension in my vagina, like after my surgery in the United States. It's a little uncomfortable. I sit on a bench and I write, relaxing. An hour passes, and as I walk to the bookstore (curious to see if I can find any information about Dr. Augusto,) my lower tummy starts to hurt. I try to ignore it. I find a paragraph on Dr. Augusto: "Not much is known about the young Brazilian doctor. He was very picky, cautious during his surgeries, and often scouted others. He was a perfectionist."

I feel pain, now in my lower back. I decide I need to go back to my room. I feel pain at the site of my surgery three and a half months ago, on my lower back and discomfort in my vagina. By the time I lie down, I really don't feel well. My arms and legs are kind of clumsy. I felt cramps, again like three and a half months ago. I take a Pepto-Bismol. I'm starting to freak out. What is happening to me?

It's lunchtime, but I feel nauseous. I can't think of eating. I force myself to eat some crackers and drink some Gatorade. Mid afternoon, feeling very cold, I walk out of the room to lie in the sun. I'm scared of being alone. My neighbor, a woman who doesn't speak English, is reading outside. I signal that I'm cold, not feeling well, and stand in the sun. I warm up some, but still don't feel well. I lie on a hammock, and after a while I feel better. By the end of the afternoon I lie in bed with a lot of discomfort around my vagina. The tension feels just like the month after the surgery when the doctor said there was still lots of inflammation.

Why do I hurt so much now? It doesn't make any sense. I walk to the refrigerator on the patio and get ice cubes, put them in a plastic bag, and use it to numb the pain. I pass by the mirror and notice how bad I look. Pale, scared, frowning. It's 7:00 p.m. I can hear my neighbors going to dinner. I don't feel hungry at all, but I know I need to eat. I sit for a minute but need to lie down again. At 7:30 I make myself go to the restaurant area. I make a plate and force the food and water down. I'm not well. I'm scared, not knowing why I feel so bad. Could it be from the spiritual surgery? But that was last Thursday, 5 days ago!

Mr. Noberto, the inn owner, walks by and I ask, "Mr. Noberto could we talk for a minute?"

"Good night," he says, and walks away.

I ask the front desk guy to call Ricardo. I tell him what is going on. I am now crying, and he tells me, "I explained to you this could happen after spiritual surgery."

"No, you didn't. I'm scared, alone, and in pain," I cry.

He says he will see me the next day. I feel helpless. Sobbing, I sit down again.

Valdete, Mr. Noberto's wife, is sitting on the other side of the room. She walks over to me. "It's okay. If you need to you can talk to one of us." I say, "I tried, didn't you hear? Even just now, I asked Mr. Noberto for a minute, and he walked away saying good night. I am confused, scared, in pain."

She tells me this is all normal. I should drink lots of water, pray, and let it pass until my "stitches" are removed on the eighth day. I cry and cry. I pass by the chapel, kneel by the amethyst crystal, and say a prayer to feel better. I go back to my room to take a shower, drink more water, and go to bed. By 9:00 p.m. the pain is gone from the stomach and the vaginal discomfort has mostly disappeared. I fall asleep.

In the middle of the night the woman in the next room screams, then silence. She must have had a nightmare. I remember the guard of our house when I was a teenager. He used to say that I scared him many nights when I talked and screamed in my sleep. It took a while, but I went back to sleep again.

"It's the unknown that draws people." — E.A. Bucchianeri

FEELING MORE AT EASE WITH "IT" ALL

I wake up feeling well! Tired, sleepy, but well. I can smile, as long as I don't dwell on what happened the day before. I feel a little embarrassed by the crying scene at the restaurant, but luckily the only people there were a couple and a worker. I hoped not to see any of them at breakfast, and to my relief they weren't there. I left a note for Valdete, thanking her for the comforting words, and I walked to the Casa.

I walked to the wooden triangle that hangs on a wall, press my forehead on the center as I have seen people doing, and say a prayer for myself. As I walk away, I see that a dozen people are peeling and cutting a ton of vegetables. I ask if I can help.

"Yes. Put some gloves on, get a knife, and you can help that woman cut the winter squash for the free soup to be served tomorrow."

Lawrence is from north of Toulouse, France. She shares that she lived in the United States for a year, a long time ago. When we finish our work we walk and sit on a bench, waiting for her crystal bed session. I briefly tell her what happened yesterday. This is her second time here in Abadiânia. She tells me it's all side effects of my spiritual surgery.

"It happens like this a lot of times, but everyone is different. Even if you had your physical surgery three and a half months ago, some stuff can be left behind and that's what the spiritual surgery is for."

"But during the spiritual surgery, the only thing I felt was the sensation that a straw was inserted on my head, directly above the right eye, and then my forehead felt really strange."

"Yes, I felt the same," she said. "That was the anesthetic going in, so you wouldn't feel pain."

"What the heck? I guess it makes some sense. At least all of 'this' didn't only happen to me."

I know this is all bizarre, but real. Yep, real! I finish writing at the garden, on a bench under the mango tree. I now know I'm okay. I have been here for one week now. I walked around a bit to get to know the town. I visited other inns. I had lunch at Fruits: tall passion fruit and mango juice and a hot sandwich. Very nice setting with shaded patio and open air. There's soft music, which offers a nice vibe.

There's a sing-along at 3:00 p.m. by the soup kitchen at the Casa. I really enjoy this. It feels good, light, and right. I go. I sing. I flow.

I am starting to realize that this place invites one to holistically care for the self. Meditation, healthy food, walks, human interaction, and a healing vibe... all at a very affordable price for room and board.

August 7, 2013 – Second Week at The Casa Starts

I wake up to another beautiful day. The mornings and nights are a little cold, the days just warm enough to be comfortable. The breakfast area and patio at the inn are filled with people in white clothing by 6:40 a.m. At 7:10 a.m. I enter the Casa main hall; most of the chairs are already taken. I sit on a side bench not far from the small stage and meditate. At 7:20 a.m., the people on the already long line go in to start "working" in the current rooms, praying, and meditating for all. They will be there, eyes closed, for at least 4 hours.

At 8:15 a.m., volunteers of the Casa start to explain procedures. João de Deus comes to the stage for the voluntary "physical surgeries." He performs them for a variety of people, scraping eyes with a small kitchen knife, or inserting a surgical instrument into the nostrils. Not a single person appears to feel discomfort! The entity sometimes has a bit of an attitude, warning that if there's too much noise he will ascend. However, most of the time kindness emanates on his face, even through the eyes, which appear on a trance.

Suddenly, the entity turns around and says, "All of you with AIDS, cancer, or peptic ulcer, who want 'surgery', come in now. Forget your line; just come in if you want to be cured. But you have to promise you will come back in 5 years with the medical proof of your cure. If you can't give me that, don't come in."

Then he adds, "There are no secrets here about your condition. Don't be embarrassed."

Quite a few people move right along. We are told that it's unusual for so many operations to be performed in such a short period. I'm confused if I should go or not, so I don't.

When the second line is called, I go in, hoping I can ask something. But as soon as I say, "I had spiritual surgery last week," he says, "I know. Go receive a pass."

I'm disappointed, but as soon as I close my eyes I think of Bruno coming out of me when I was 8 months pregnant and I cry all over again. I'm still grieving after almost 25 years! I learned from Louise Hay first, and then others, that cancer can be caused by deep grief, resentment, and/or guilt. Is that why Bruno is coming up?

I guess I still haven't fully let my son go, as I had thought I did. I am thinking about him often here in Abadiânia. I remember the guru I met in Bali last year. He didn't know me at all and I had not shared anything personal with anyone in Bali, when he asked me, "You have two kids, right?" The guru in Bali, who didn't know me at all, had said a year ago, "You have two kids, right?" I nodded confirming. He went on, "But you have the third one who is no longer here. You have to let him go."

The blood left my face. I was so shocked. He is talking about Bruno. How could he know? I say, "What are you talking about? I let him go, a long time ago."

"No, you haven't," he tells me. "I can see him by your side. You have to let him go."

So, here in Abadiânia, I cry all over again, and I realize that despite a span of a quarter century, I am still grieving my son.

August 8, 2013 – Spiritual Stitches Removed

Morning starts as the days before, waking up early at 6:00 a.m., but this time I drink the cup of blessed water by my bed first, before getting up. My "spiritual stitches" had been removed the night before.

After breakfast I head to the Casa where I take a free "revision" ticket. When revision line is called, I go in and am told by the entity, "I will help you."

In the afternoon, I go to the prayer current room again. As I close my eyes I see the color blue most of the time. Now my whole hands feels hot, not just the center of the palms. Four and a half hours pass. As usual, the current ends with a couple of prayers in Portuguese, a thank you, and we're given a tiny cup of blessed water as we walk out.

I walk to the inn, now waving "hellos" to people I already know: Enrique, the Brazilian with a walker or wheelchair/tricycle; the man from Palo Alto and his daughter; Doug from Southern California; Sergio and his daughter Tatiana and little son; Russians from Canada, et cetera.

Sergio is a doctor who has been here six times during the past 17 months with his son who is ill, cute and extremely active. According to his dad, the boy's improvement has been remarkable. He now talks and is much calmer. After the first visit here, also in the company of the child's mother (who also is a physician), the improvement was already amazing. He says he told the teachers at the daycare in Canada that they had gone to Russia, but they were actually here.

I meet my brother in the evening. He'll be here for a few days. This is his first time here, so I gave a brief introduction to the rhythm of the Casa. The doctrine behind it, I don't have to describe as he has been studying "spiritism" for some years and understands it perfectly. I am the one who feels like I am in kindergarten, without much understanding of it all.

August 9, 2013 – My Brother Meets Me at The Casa

I'm headed to the Casa at 7:00 a.m., this time with my brother. I got a second-time pass for me, and a first-time ticket for him. John of God doesn't come out this morning. He saw people inside, one by one, as they came through the continuous lines.

Approximately 600 people are seen in the morning, 600 in the afternoon, 3 days per week. He only finishes when all are seen. I kneel before the healer and he agrees that I should sit in the healing current in his room. I see my brother already sitting there, eyes closed. This is a short session, ending at 11:00 a.m. I can hear complaints that people are coming in on the wrong lines. Discipline is demanded here. The work is finished an hour before it usually does.

When afternoon arrives, I am finally exhausted and decide to stay in my room, doing yoga, reading, listening to music, and then showering.

August 10-12 - Weekend with Family

I leave Abadiânia and visit relatives in Goiânia, which is an hour and a half away. I haven't seen my aunt and cousins for 30 years. I have a great time, but miss the vibe around the Casa. I'm eager to return to its surroundings and high healing energy.

August 13 - Another Cat Enters My Life

I arrive back in Abadiânia and check in at Inn São Miguel. There is an absolutely gorgeous tri-colored cat with aqua-colored eyes at the entrance.

My sister-in-law says, "That's your cat."

"No. I have enough cats already." I say joking.

After dinner, I go to Pousada Brasil to chat with my brother. It's 9:00 p.m. when I leave and my pousada's lights are already off. As I get to the inside garden patio, I see "my" cat sitting on a wooden bench. As I pass, he jumps off and starts to walk by my side. Then he's in front of my feet, going around between my legs, rubbing against my pants.

When I get to my room the cat sits by me, staring at the door. I stand there for a few minutes and it sits between my legs. I decide to walk to the front patio to see if I can leave him (her) there. The cat buddy rubbed my legs all the way there. The owner of the pousada took him. Next day he shares that the cat appeared there 2 days before with no owner. That's the day I arrived, too. Hum!

Wednesday morning the cat is at the entrance of the dining area at 7:00 a.m. and at the exit when I pass at 7:15 a.m. By Thursday I see the cat every time I go in and out. On Friday, I give in. I sit on the wooden bench, and she jumps to my side. It's the first time I touch a cat in my life and let it sit on my lap.

I'm puzzled and I felt it was time for me to Google the meaning of *cat*, as someone had suggested I do. "Guardian; brings out intuition; connects one to the outer world; nine lives." Hum!

August 14, 2013 – Third Week at The Casa

Breakfast at 8 a.m. A tasty variety of food is served buffet style. For about $47 a day we get a simple but nice and clean room, and 3 full and delicious meals. Tons of food is served at each meal, plus fresh juices, fresh herb teas, coffee, and dessert.

The session in the main hall starts late. I take the time to close my eyes and just let it be. When it starts, I stand in line to go before the entity, holding a picture of the Balinese boy and a tiny one of my friend Helen, who was recovering from knee surgery in Australia and was experiencing lots of pain. Once inside, I must confess I focus on asking for blessing for Komang, on asking that I continue to find sick children to help, and asking for clarity about my premonition dreams. Helen isn't on my mind while I'm in line.

I feel the back of both of my knees burning. It's really painful but I tell myself, "How unusual; I have never had pain in my legs, of any type, let alone in my knees."

When my turn comes, I ask John of God for continuing health improvement for the boy, that I find more children in need and for Helen's healing, as I handed him the pictures. "I want to see you in the afternoon. Go get a pass." the entity says. And so I did.

It isn't until later, once out of the Casa, that I think that the burning behind my knees could have been related to Helen's knees. I had forgotten about her problem while in line. And another *hum* crosses my mind.

In the afternoon, I arrive at the Casa's main hall at 1:15 p.m. and get a middle aisle seat. Soon after a woman carrying a baby passes by and I give her my seat. I sit on the floor.

Her line is called and I get the seat back. A couple of minutes later a man walking with a cane passes by and I offer my seat again. Back to the floor I go, until his line is called and I take the seat for the third time. Yet another elderly man passes by and I give up the seat once again.

A Brazilian woman a few seats away says, "Oh, my God. You're here to serve. I saw all three people walking all over the hall looking for a seat, and each time you were the only one to offer yours."

I stay in the main hall all afternoon, listening to testimonials and observing the continuous flow of people coming in, hour after hour. The diversity of cultures and backgrounds was amazing and so unusual to be found in Brazil.

At the end of the day, as I walk into the dining hall at my inn, the same woman points to me, saying to her friends in Portuguese, "That's the woman who had the offering seat." I smile, and she says she thought I was a foreigner.

I share that I'm from Maceió, Brazil, but that I live in the United States. She adds, "I only know one person in Maceió, Lurdinha Lyra."

I burst, "No way. I know her. Actually, I met her four months ago in Maceió." We smile, very surprised…or not. Synchronicity, Dr. Weiss would probably say.

August 15, 2013 – Learning More About Spiritism

In the afternoon, I go in carrying pictures of my sister and two nephews. I kneel and say I am asking for two family members from Maceio. The entity looks at me. "Daughter, where do you live?" I answer, "In the United States, but I have family in Maceió." He keeps the pictures, gives prescriptions for all 3, and asks that I get a pass.

Outside, I talk to Heather, asking where I can get answers about my dreams, intuitions, and coincidences. I'm told to wait for the medium by the back door to see if he would talk to me after the session. I don't feel comfortable bothering him after such a long day. So I didn't.

My brother is a spiritist (one who believes in spirits, the souls which live on after death and have the ability to communicate with enlightened humans). He studies spiritism deeply as a philosophy, and now tries to pass lots of information to me. Many times I tell him to slow down. I can't go that deep yet. Too much has happened, and I still can't grasp it all. He says he is jealous of my intuition and wishes he had a fraction of it. He can't believe that I still need more proof! He keeps asking me, "How many cats do you need to start believing?" I shrug and smile each time.

The saying "Faith is to believe in what you don't see," is repeated many times here, but I AM NOT READY to embrace that yet.

I don't necessarily need more proof but need more answers. I'm told that I have a third eye, which I need to open. What does that mean? What will be unleashed? My brother says, "If you open it up you will need to be ready, and to dedicate more of yourself to the call." Like Dona J., who is a wealthy woman from Maceió, who for years has devoted her life to work as a medium, to heal the sick in ICUs. No social life at all. All she does is work for free as a healing medium.

I'm committed to healing myself and to love myself more, as many have told me lately that I need to do. I still don't know how I can help others more by using mediumship. I don't have it. I don't even understand it.

That's what I have been hearing since Omega in New York, that I'm a medium! That sounds strange to me still. This is the very first time I'm acknowledging that I might, just maybe, be one. I've read that everyone is a medium (intuitive), but some are more developed. Okay. If everyone is one, that's easier to accept that I might be one too.

August 16, 2013 – Meaningful Encounters at The Casa

My brother has left to Goiânia. I join the current line at 7:15 a.m. I enjoy the instructions and words of the Irish woman who volunteers to lead the first current room. Eyes closed to do the "work," which lasts 4 hours.

At 11:30 a.m. I have the free and delicious bowl of vegetable soup sitting by a gorgeous blonde young woman.

"I know you, but I don't know from where." She says to me with a big smile.

"No, I don't think we have met before," I say. "Where are you from?"

"I live in Maui, Hawaii, and you?"

I tell her, "Gainesville, Florida."

"Ah, I have a cousin in Jacksonville, near Gainesville."

I tell her that's where my daughter lives. Then I have déjà vu. "Now I remember. I saw you on the first-time line from across the main hall. You looked very anxious, nervous, and I smiled at you and gave you the thumbs up. You smiled back showing relief in your face."

"Ah, yes," she says. "I remember now. Thank you. I have anxiety and I was so nervous. My mom had eye melanoma ten years ago and now the cancer is back, all over her liver and lungs. She was given a couple of months to live and there is no treatment option for her. Many people told her to come see John of God, and we got every penny we had and came."

We chat for a while. She works at a resort and also as a surfing instructor in Maui. She points out that the money in my pocket is about to fall out. I put it inside my bag. As we say goodbye she gives me her email address and asks that we stay in touch. (We are still in touch as I write. Her Mom passed 1 year after Abadiânia visit). I wish her and her mom well and hand her twenty bucks.

"This is for a crystal bed for you and one for your mom."

"You don't have to," she says.

"I know, but I want to." We hug and say goodbye.

Later, we meet and she tells me she booked the crystal bed sessions and her mom was very thankful. In the afternoon, I stay at the main hall for a while and go to the waterfall later in the afternoon.

I leave for the weekend. On Monday morning, the girl touches my shoulder at the Casa's garden. We take a picture together and hug, with her promising she will send me updates.

Over lunch, I meet Fatima, a Brazilian from Uberaba, Minas Gerais. And also a mother and daughter pair, Russians living in New York, who speak Portuguese fluently.

During dinner we sit together and chat. It feels like we've met before. The conversation flows effortlessly. Fatima has been to the Casa many times before and she is knowledgeable about spiritism. Later, chatting on the porch, she tells me she used to be exactly like me: fearful and shy about her natural ability as a medium, one who could "see" a lot. The future? The past? Hmm. A medium? Me? No way

August 17, 2013 – More Happenings on a Non-Casa Day

The four of us have breakfast together and Fatima shares more about spiritism. She shares books and experiences she has lived. I have a crystal bed session and feel strong sensations on my forehead and nose. I also feel a band across my chest, and again, it doesn't make any sense to me. Later I'm told my heart chakra is opening. At the Casa garden a young guy approaches me. He walks with much difficulty, but I've been told he was rude when help was offered to him. He asks me to write something in English for him. He says he spends most days at home and learned English from movies. This is his first visit to the Casa, and he feels better.

I tell him I've seen him around.

"What did you think of me?"

"You seem unhappy," I tell him.

"Yes, I am unhappy. I feel I'm losing my body."

I ask what illness he has. "I don't know. The doctors don't find any reason."

I say, "You are feeling better here. Be grateful for what you have - sight, intelligence - and ask for what you need."

A woman nearby nods in agreement. She comes closer. It's his mother. He asks if he can touch my hair, and I agree. We pose for a picture and say goodbye. The young man and his mom look happier as they walk away.

Back at the inn I finish packing to go to Morrinhos with my brother to visit a second cousin and his partner, at a farm by a lovely river.

August 18, 2013 – Day Visiting Friends

I spend time at the farm and Goiânia. So nice seeing the love at Pa's full home. There are eight, including Du, who has Down syndrome, plus three guests. In the evening we drive to Abadiânia. As I arrive at the Pousada São Miguel, "my cat" is waiting at the entrance. I go in, meditate, read and go to sleep. I love it here.

"The universe is always speaking to us... sending us little messages, causing coincidences and serendipities, reminding us to stop, to look around, to believe in something else, something more." — Nancy Thayer

Unbelievable Encounter with a Clairvoyant and a Scary Night

Breakfast is at 8:00 a.m. with my Russian friends. Then I head to the Casa for a crystal bed session. It is relaxing. I still feel a strong sensation between my eyes but it doesn't matter; I feel great here.

At lunch, I greet an older man who has just arrived at the inn, and ask if he's American. "Canadian." He answers.

I head to the table at the veranda I have been sharing with the Russian ladies. We speak in Portuguese so they can practice it. The Canadian gentleman is siting at the table next to ours, with his wife. We introduce ourselves and I ask if it is their first time here.

"This is our twelfth time! We have been coming since 2009."

We all went, "Twelve?" in disbelief. We have met people who had come 3, 4, and up to 6 times, but 12!

I ask what brought them back so many times. He says that the time before last, John of God had operated on him, physically. On his head, removing 4 pea-size tumors!

We ask if it hurt, without any anesthesia. He said "No, not at all." and added that he had pictures to prove. We ask to see them. He goes to his room to get the photos and brings them to our table. Wow!! His face is serene, and John of God's eyes, are mostly closed, while he is cutting and also stitching the Warren's head.

We then asked Sylvia, the wife, if she wanted to join us. She comes, and still standing, and without warning, she turns to Marina and says, "I can see the baby who was miscarried."

"I didn't have a miscarriage." shares Marina, surprised.

Sylvia says, "Someone close to you did. He is here. I can see him. It's a boy."

Sylvia is now looking at the space between Marina and I. With a faint voice, I say, "I had a stillborn boy."

"He wants me to tell you that he loves you very much and that he waited until you were ready, to move on to another plane. It is time for him to go." says the woman, still standing.

I turn pale. Marina holds my hand. Sylvia moves around the small table and stands besides me, adding, with a smile: "He wants you to know that he always felt your love and that he is very glad you got the puppy he wanted you to get. He loves to play with him".

What? How does she know I adopted a pet, a puppy, which happens to be a male? How? I remember that I often think of Bruno, my angel son, when I play with Ziggy, my puppy. I am in disbelief, shocked. I just met this woman a few minutes ago, and I haven't shared absolutely anything with anybody here about the son I lost or about my puppy. How can she know? How?

It was hard to let go of what happened. I remember the guru in Bali telling me that I had to let go of my son, that he could see him by my side, although I didn't know him and he didn't know anything about me either. I remember scattering my son's ashes at Epcot Center, thinking that it was the "let go." Now I hear that he is finally "ready to go", because now I am ready. Lots to be wrapped around my head. How can this stranger, from a different part of the world, know about Bruno and can see him? How?

Later in the day, after dinner, I go for a walk with Marisha, the younger Russian woman. I shared how I lost my first child, so unexpectedly. She is also at awe about what happened over lunch with the clairvoyant. I am starting to believe that I don't have a choice, but to accept all these happenings as not just surreal, but actually real.

I go to bed at 9:30 p.m. I put on a relaxation app, but it keeps stopping. It doesn't make sense that the downloaded apps won't work, as no Internet is needed. I tried to open links on YouTube, but all of them keep stopping too, although the Wi-Fi has a strong signal. So I give up and go to sleep.

In the middle of the night, I wake up with my own scream. I open my eyes to find myself at the very edge of the bed, tummy down and touching the bed, but my head and feet are suspended up, off the mattress. My left arm is hanging off the bed and my right arm feels frozen at my side. I try to move but can't. I'm inert! It's so scary. I am not dreaming. I am certain of that. What is going on? What?

All of a sudden I am able to move, and I push myself from the edge of the bed. I am scared, puzzled. I look at the clock and it's 2:35 a.m. I can't sleep for the rest of the night. What a bizarre thing! I can't wait for the sun to rise so I can get out of this room.

August 20, 2013 – Around Abadiânia

Morning comes at last, and I head out for breakfast. I share what happened with Marina and Marisha, expecting to hear that this was just a dream or something like that. Instead, I'm told, "Oh. You had an out-of-body experience. Yes, you couldn't move because your spirit wasn't in your body. Was it between 2:00 and 4:00 a.m.?" I nod affirming.

"That's when spirits are active and do their work. John of God wakes up to pray every day at 2am."

Yes, this is all so new to me, and I'm puzzled and still scared.

"Nothing to fear", she says.

My Russian and Austrian friends join me at the Casa at 8:30 a.m. to help prepare the vegetables for the free and delicious soup that The Casa's kitchen serves to all, free of charge. That keeps my mind off the bizarre happenings.

Later we walk about 30 minutes to the other side of town, where the locals live and the Casa has a soup kitchen for them. The place is spotless. In addition to 1,500 bowls of soup served per day, homemade fruit popsicles are also served for free. Upstairs there is a donation center with clothing and school supplies. The soup/donation center is sustained by donations from the Casa.

Visitors to the Casa make donations that are neatly organized and distributed once per week. Gowns and fancier clothing hang from a rack. These special occasion items are lent, not given away. Upstairs there is also a meditation/meeting room.

João de Deus's home is in front of the blue distribution building, and he often comes by. On Fridays, it is Senior Day. There's dancing and João de Deus even throws money up in the air for whoever grabs it. There are pictures on the wall, including of some famous people. We stroll around little stores and get back to the inn just in time for lunch.

At 3:00 p.m., it's sing-along time, to the sound of guitars. I really enjoy this weekly one-hour activity! Then, I am invited to visit a gorgeous house across from the Casa, which belongs to a Russian man, Glenn, who works in healthcare in New Jersey. The view is amazing and so is the hospitality. Five of us chat over a delicious watermelon. At 6:00 p.m., yet another delicious dinner, with tons of nutritious food at the inn. And so ends another fulfilling day in Abadiânia.

August 21, 2013 – Finally Comfortable with "It All" at the Casa

I'm up at 6:00 a.m., and at 6:45 a.m. I'm headed to the Casa. I join the current line, which has already formed. Many carry pillows for more comfort during the four to six hour meditation sessions. A woman from Boston is behind me. She shares that she isn't sick, but she heard of John of God and felt she belonged here.

Already in the current room, I suddenly hear John of God's voice say, "Your father needs help. As for you, I've already done all I could."

With my eyes closed I see white floaters coming at me. Beautiful shapes. I think of Bruno, my son.

Around 11:40 a.m. I join the soup line and enjoy a bowl of soup as a snack. At 12:30 p.m. I'm having lunch. Yes, I consume a lot of food here, but mainly fresh and nutritious dishes made with vegetables.

At 5:00 p.m. I have another 20-minute crystal bed session in room No. 11. First, I see nothing, then a single eye. It stares at me, wide open. Its color is hazel. It looks like a younger eye than the parade of old eyes, most half closed, I have been seeing during the past three and a half weeks, while meditating here at the Casa.

Suddenly, I think and know in my heart they are Bruno's eyes. My baby. Tears run down my cheeks as I recall saying and writing that I never got to see his eyes, since he was born dead and his eyes were closed. Now I see his beautiful hazel eyes. I am crying out of happiness. A little later I feel my third eye area gently tense, unlike other times.

At 5:30 p.m. I share my session with Marisha and Marina and we take a taxi to the waterfall. Again I perform the little ceremony by the entrance, a circle with a hand giving, and the other receiving. At the first bridge I let go of the past, at the second the present, and at the third I see the future. Under the very cold cleansing water I receive light, energy, health, hope, happiness, and cleansing of negativity. I want to move forward and out to give light, hope, and positivity. I repeat the ritual one more time.

After helping Marina, who can't see without her glasses, we walk back. We feel refreshed and not cold, despite the fact that the water was super cold and the orange sun is already setting beautifully behind the gentle rolling hills. I silently thank the Universe for another sublime time.

August 22, 2013 – Nice and Happy Day

I've slept well the past two nights. After breakfast, I head to the crystal bed for a 40-minute double session. I lay down under the flickering colored lights, each with a clear crystal underneath, I start to breathe very rapidly and deeply. My whole chest area begins to feel very hot, as if I had a hot water bottle across it.

By now I know that the area corresponds to the heart chakra. After a while I see one hazel eye. I smile, still amazed by the intense heat in the heart area.

I can hear the birds singing outside, and red color takes over my sight, with the eyes closed. I see an arm extended, holding a gun! Just for a second. That's strange, but I don't dwell on it.

The current lasts 4 hours. Surprisingly my shoulders and neck do not bother me at all. I am relaxed. I see a few eyes and faces even though my eyes are closed. I feel heat on the palms of my hands, which is common now. At the end of each current, we get a chance to receive energy and prayers.

71

As soon as the current is over I head to the waterfall. The ceremony by the three bridges, the cold cleansing water, all feels so right. Surprisingly, I love the freezing water, and tolerate the cold super well. It's so refreshing, and it feels like a spiritual blessing. As I leave, the sun sets behind a mountain. Beautiful! I walk the dirt road silently feeling so light and at peace, arriving at the inn as dinner is served.

August 23, 2013 – Last Day in Abadiânia

Today is my last day at Abadiânia. After breakfast at 6:55 a.m. with Marina and Marisha, I head to the current line at the Casa, which is already long at 7:15 a.m. It lasts about four and a half hours. Primarily foreigners fill the first current room.

I have lunch, have a crystal bed session, and then it's back at the main hall at 1:15 p.m. I sit near the front, by a Brazilian family from the state of Mato Grosso. It's their first time. They are confused, uncertain about what to do and impressed by the number of foreigners. I guide them.

The session starts unusually late.

I drop by an Internet café near my inn. A tall, American man around 70 years old is ticked because he can't close or save a picture he said he took 2 weeks before. It's a picture taken inside the room where people who have had "physical" operations go. It shows some people lying in bed, a couple of people (volunteers) attending to them, and a few others, with faded images of their bodies: the spirits that were present, I'm told. I ask and get a copy of the picture. I'll ask my sister, who is a photographer, if it seems real. I just have to.

Dinner is a full table at the inn, as five other Russians joined us. It is a lively time. Four live in the United States and one in Scandinavia. The woman, an engineer, shares an interesting, and even funny, story about two women friends of hers who came to Abadiânia. One wanted to come because of her eyesight. She was a former professional biker who had to retire because of poor vision, due to an unusual disorder. Her friend was a non-believer, sarcastic about the whole spirit thing, but had decided to come along. She'd been having abdominal pain lately. They both had spiritual surgery, and

72

the biker insisted on following all the protocols, like taking a taxi to the inn after surgery and staying in bed for 24 hours. She says she improved overnight. The skeptical one left the Casa saying she didn't feel anything and making fun of the whole thing.

The next morning, however, the skeptic freaked out when she found that her legs were incredibly swollen and she had shortness of breath. She could barely walk. She then realized that it was probably not her abdomen that was operated on, but her heart, as she had a heart condition as a child.

She followed protocol from this point on, and at the revision line before the entity she could barely walk or stand. A few feet from the entity, she felt a rush of energy pouring over her and suddenly felt well. She screamed in happiness, causing a scene.

As the two women headed to the airport (they were in Abadiânia only for a week) the skeptic said she was feeling great but the other one was disappointed because her vision had worsened again, and her sight was very poor.

So, the story goes, at the airport at the X-ray machine, she was told her two-liter water bottle (with blessed water) can't go through. She created a scene to no avail. It was not allowed to go through. She refused to leave it. Because she was holding up the line, and decided to drink the whole thing, pouring water all over herself in the process. As she finished she passed the security checkpoint and realized that she could see clearly again. This happened a couple of years ago and she can still see well, according to the Russian telling the story.

Someone shares a similar story. The entity was performing a physical surgery on stage, and he turns to the audience and points to a Russian man. "You are a doctor. Come to stand by me." The doctor, surprised, walks to the stage, standing where he could see the person being operated on, slightly behind the medium. He watches the body of the volunteer being cut. When the entity starts to stitch the incision, the doctor thinks to himself, "That's not how I stitch. This is wrong." The entity immediately turns around and says, "I used to stitch the way you do years ago. This way is better." The doctor is shocked, spooked, because his mind was read. Also, there's hardly any blood on the patient and he doesn't seem to have any discomfort at all.

Stories like this are common here, being told by the "patient" him/ herself or by people who witness or know someone who had a miracle happen: spontaneous healing and disappearance of tumors, AIDS patients surviving for decades, people getting out of wheelchairs. Many don't get fully healed but express their happiness with the great improvement of their health and well being, like my new friend Henrique. He is a 60-year-old man with many health problems. He has chronic kidney failure and walks with a walker. He told me he was here 2 years ago, got much better and returned home. He got worse again and returned to Abadiânia 9 months ago, and has been calling it home ever since.

"Why I am still here? I feel better here. Why would I leave?" he tells me with a smile. His beautiful stepdaughter is here to get a blessing before she moves to Australia. Her mom, his wife, has died.

Warren comes into the dining room and tells me Sylvia, the clairvoyant, would like to say goodbye to me but she can't leave her room. So I go there. She says how happy she is to see me, and that "Bruno was here in a sailor suit, waving goodbye. He's happy and well. He looks older." A tear, not of sorrow, rolls down my face. I'm okay, too. Sylvia asks if I will be in touch. I say yes, and we hug, wishing each other well.

August 23, 2013 – Oh! I'm Leaving Abadiânia on Another 23!

This is my last day in Abadiânia, but I already bought a ticket to return in 38 days, October 1, so I'm not really sad, just aware that I'll miss the friends who won't be here then. But this is the nature of this place: Thousands of people coming and going each week. I say goodbye to the Russian "family," like Glenn called us, to Marco, to Karla, to Enrique. At 11:00 p.m. Marina and Marisha come to my room and help me carry my bags to the taxi, including the pretty and heavy crystal I purchased.

The cat "waited" for me up front. We say goodbye, the four of us (including the cat). We had become a team, an extended family. By 1:15 a.m. I am at the Brasilia airport for the 2:30 a.m. flight to Panama City, where I connect to Orlando.

August 24, 2013 – Another Plane Seatmate Connected to Gainesville

About 45 minutes before landing, the gentleman by my side compliments my reading glasses, adding that his wife is an ophthalmologist. I say that I just got a message to call my ophthalmologist. He is coming from Paraguay, lives in DC, and is on his way to visit his daughter who moved to Orlando a year ago. She is a nurse practitioner working in oncology! I briefly share that I have been around many oncologists lately.

He asks if I live in Orlando. "No, Gainesville, a couple of hours north."

He says, "Oh well. I was born in Gainesville and went to the university there!"

"No way," I say. I can't believe it! Another flight seated by someone from Gainesville. It's all so odd, these "coincidences." He is the fifth one, just recently.

We go on to talking about "my cats," his motorcycle, family, and travels.

A couple of days later he writes me saying that he enjoyed the chat, wishes me good health, and hopes he will come by on his motorcycle someday.

*"I must be willing to give up what I am in
order to become what I will be."*
— Albert Einstein

BACK HOME, IT'S NOT EASY AT FIRST

Back home, but I miss the vibe of Abadiânia. It was so much easier to be surrounded by people who "understood" what I am just beginning to understand about true healing, life, and death.

The few friends who know I was in Brazil are curious to know how it was. I give a synopsis of what it is like there and show pictures, but to understand "it" fully, one must be there and see and feel it all.

To my happy surprise, Yannick, my 17-year-old son, has been the most supportive and interested in my accountings of the Casa. My husband listened at first, but with no real interest. Amanda tries to be open and supportive, but isn't really engaged; she has a "good that you found it helpful but not for me," kind of attitude. So, I feel alone on this new path, at least at home.

Five days after my return, I get sick with stomach flu. I have nausea and weakness. It lasts 4 days. It's so hard to relax. One day I actually break down in tears. I can't stop sobbing. I feel overwhelmed. It's so strange after being in such bliss just a few days before. I feel helpless for some hours. But thank God, the day when I seem back to myself arrives and I feel grateful.

August 31, 2013 – Another Friend Diagnosed with Cancer

I got an unexpected message from a friend I went to school with at University of California, Davis, about 28 years ago. She wanted to reconnect after many years. I answered saying I was working less due a cancer diagnosis. To my even greater surprise, I get this news: "I am so sorry to hear of your cancer dx! I too have recently been diagnosed with cancer (non-small cell lung cancer). I added you to my private Facebook cancer group so you can see my posts. How can it be that we both have cancer??? I am looking forward to hearing all about your life and travels - sounds so exciting! Talk to you soon. Xoxo Melisa." How can it be that we both have cancer? Melisa is also a dietitian, thin, athletic, a mother of two, has a love for animals and life. Oh, life. Oh the Universe. What do you have in store for us? My dear Chester, Melisa, and I, all three with cancer! Why? What lessons are to be learned by us?

*"Loving yourself does not mean being self-absorbed,
it means welcoming yourself as the most honored
guest in your own heart."* — Margo Anand

CONTINUING TO LEARN HOW TO HEAL THE SPIRITUAL CAUSES OF ILLNESS

I have no doubt that the treatment of cancer, and many other chronic diseases, requires a holistic approach. At the moment I don't have any active "dis-ease" the doctors can detect and treat, but my mind and spirit still need to be cared for.

I've continued to work on trying to achieve a true relaxed state, still needing guidance, relying on YouTube and app-guided meditations. I finally get around to Googling Dr. Wayne Dyer, as he was suggested to me at Omega and he was mentioned at the Casa as one of those cured of Leukemia through a spiritual surgery from the Entities of the Casa. On YouTube, I see he is a great match to my needs and he *gets to the point* easily. He summarizes, in a simplistic way, what I have been hearing or reading or seeing during the past two months, and what I have observed with Buddhism as well. (I have backpacked through all Himalayan Buddhist countries.)

Now it was time to search Louise Hay, as she has been recommended to me as well. Each of her words about healing and cancer sounds like a melody I am learning how to sing. Very helpful! Now I have a group of "healing gurus" to learn from, to be guided by.

Many friends from the Casa have been in touch. Cree found out from the address at the bottom of my email that I'm a diabetes educator and has shared that she has diabetes. We reconnect strongly. We already have the "Oh my God! I was just thinking of contacting you," whenever one messages the other.

Cree took the passiflora from the Casa to my friend Chester, who continues in treatment in Houston for the pancreatic tumor. They formed a bond instantly, just as I thought they would. That makes me so happy. How I miss my friend Chester.

September 4, 2013 – Insomnia and More Regressions

It's 3:00 a.m. and I still can't sleep. I haven't had insomnia like this in a long time. I know it's unhealthy for the body, which needs rest. I toss and turn for too long and finally decide to do my own regression, a prompt to see if I can fall asleep.

I walk through a door even before Dr. Weiss's voice finishes the passage. I'm already "seeing" who is there. I look down at my feet, and there are no shoes. It's a young woman's feet and hands; the feet are a little dirty. My skirt is of the same style as a previous regression but immediately I start to run, desperately trying to get away from animals or men.

Soon I realize I'm running from both hunting dogs and older bearded men. I'm thrown to the ground. Why? I'm tired, scared, I fall, and I'm raped by the man with the bushy black beard.

When Dr. Weiss says to move to another scene, I'm in an old dark wood cabin. It's tiny and isolated. I'm stressed as I hold and try to calm my baby daughter. She's a few months old, wearing a white baby hat tied below her neck. She is crying nonstop. Is she ill? I don't know. I'm tired. I know an older man comes by from time to time to bring food and some other supplies.

I'm between 21 and 23 years old in this regression. I don't know why I live alone and isolated. Shame? Expelled from the village? I don't know. Then I'm outside chopping firewood. It's hard. My shoulder hurts, my upper back, particularly the right side, hurts. (*Hmm, that's where I have tension, pain, and need massage.*) The next thing I know it's another day. As I'm guided to move to the end of that life, I see my body under a large, thick tree branch. Apparently, it fell across my back. I died. I immediately see my body, lying still, before Dr. Weiss even guided me to. My body is then a little older. Wearing the same hat, sitting on the ground near my dead body, unhurt, is my little girl. I see the young man, now a little older, who approaches my body, sees I'm dead, caresses my hair and goes on to

79

tend the baby. He picks her up. He isn't the father. He's the man who saved me after I almost drowned in the river, as I saw in another regression. He has silently loved me, and I knew it. But I couldn't be with anyone, only alone. Life is hard for me. Dr. Weiss says to observe if someone -- an angel, light, or observer is with me, above the ground. It's a young woman. I don't know her. I say that I can't die yet because of the baby. She says the baby will be cared for by the young man I trusted. But it breaks my heart to leave. I'm told it's my time and that I've already gone through too much struggle and sorrow.

The session ends. I'm still not sleeping and don't understand what happened. I fell in the river or tried to commit suicide? How did I end up with my grandfather in that regression? I have to find out and decide to do another regression to see if I can find out. It's 2:30 a.m. This is all so odd, I know, yet I want to understand. I begin again:

I look down at my feet and they are those of a small girl, around 5 years old. The shoes are pretty, new, expensive. I start to walk, holding my mother's hand. My dress is pretty, dark colors. I have a hat tied under my chin. My mother is elegant, slim, and tall. We are in a city. I think it's London. We arrive at a busy square. We approach a horse carriage. My mother tells the man in black clothing (he is a little older and has a distended belly and white beard and wears a tall black hat) that we are just going for a ride. The two of us hop into the seat behind the man, side by side. My mom is seated to my left. As we start to move, a black car, one of those early models, small and narrow, loses control and comes directly at us. It hits my mother's side. She falls. People gather. She is dead.

Dr. Weiss's voice guides me to go to another scene. There is sadness, confusion. I'm in a big, fancy home. It's my home. My father is thin, elegant, disturbed. He is pacing, holding a glass of scotch. He drinks a lot, every day. My grandfather is there. He's my mother's father. He and my father are having a serious talk. He tells my dad he has neglected me, and that I should not grow without love, attention, caring. He asks, begs, to take me with him, to his humble home in a village, as he promises he'll take good care of me, love me, although he can't give me luxury. My father doesn't say anything. He stands with one hand in his pocket, the other holding his drink. I'm peeking from the hallway; I want to go with my grandpa. I feel lonely and afraid in this home without my mother. My father thinks for a long time and then says, "Go, take her. I have nothing to give her anyways. Take her now." He doesn't even look at my grandpa as he says the words. I don't know if he blames me for my mother's death. But he was distant even before. He hardly talked to her or me. He introduced us at parties and then would just drink and talk to the wealthy people. He didn't say goodbye to me. The maid packed my little suitcase. I chose a few pieces of my clothing. Grandpa held my hand as we got into the black car and drove to the train station.

When Dr. Weiss says to go to the end of that life, there's a blank. But that is okay, as I have already seen my end.

September 10, 2013 – Individually Guided Regression at Home

A few times when I'm doing meditation — or meditative regression — I see a girl, between 6 and 9 years old, arriving at Ganden Monastery in Tibet. It's a marvelous building nested on top of a high mountain of the Himalayas. I have been there three times, and I often see myself behind the majestic building, by the colorful prayer flags, overlooking the valley below, when I'm doing my relaxation. I see the girl arriving, wearing dirty brown and maroon Tibetan clothing, hair undone, and then nothing else. Am I her? I don't know. Is it just my mind's imagination? I don't know.

The last day I had worked at my office, in mid-July, before I went to see Dr. Weiss, my last patient was a man I had been counseling for a couple of years. He always came with his proactive wife, who asked lots of questions. They had shared with me, previously, that while he was at the hospital, the doctor had told her his kidney tumor was serious and she should prepare for the worst. Well, later they determined that the tumor was benign, and the man is well. Following the kidney diet I prescribed, his numbers are stable and they lead a normal life. I shared with them that I was diagnosed with cancer. The wife got teary and comforted me, saying it was very important to be positive, strong, and hopeful. We ended up talking for a while, and I shared that I was probably going to Dr. Weiss's workshop (mind that it is completely unusual for me to share personal things with my patients). The woman immediately said, "Oh my God, You must go. I met him briefly on a book signing, and I guide people to do past-life regressions here in Gainesville."

How unusual is that? What a coincidence! She handed me her card and asked to talk after the workshop.

A few days later I received a card from her, and after the workshop we spoke on the phone. I said Dr. Weiss told me to go to Brazil to see John of God, and that I was going. She asked to do a regression on me after I returned. Now she is in my blue room, about to guide me through a past-life regression session. I told her that there was a girl I'd seen several times with my mind's eye, in front of the Ganden Monastery but that was all. I have no clue who she is. So, we focus on her life.

As I regress, I "see" that she lived with her mother in a small home in the valley. Her mother died and right before told her to go up the mountain to seek help at the Ganden Monastery. She arrives at the top, tired, after walking the long winding road. An old monk sees her first. He takes her in. The elder monk is very gentle to me (her). I was given a small room with a narrow bed. It is dark, but there is a little window and yak butter lamp. I feel safe but miss my mother, and there is sadness deep within my heart. I play behind the monastery, where the colorful prayer flags flutter with the wind, sending prayers to the sky and beyond. I send prayers to my mother.

I have been to this place three times in this lifetime, and I often find myself going there during meditation. I picture myself floating above, suspended in the air, giving or receiving light from my open arms. I've also "gone" here during my CT scans. I feel at home when I "fly" here in my mind. I have never understood why.

The elder monk and another monk call me for a talk. They tell me I can't stay at the monastery because they are all males, but they know of a nunnery where the nuns will take me in, they are sure.

Two days later the three of us walk for a long time, stopping by the side of the road to eat and drink yak butter tea. The sun has come down by the time we arrive. The nuns take me in. I grew up at the nunnery. I help with chores. I'm treated very well. I'm loved, and I feel at home. But I do not become a nun. I meet a young man from the nearby village. We like each other. We plan to get married soon. We get married, and I am happy. I give birth to a child. I don't remember anything else. I am brought back.

I wanted to find out why I have chronic insomnia. So, again, I regress:

I am a girl. My name is Hope. I'm brought to live with my old and rich aunt Ann-Marie after my mother dies. I don't know about my father. My aunt is austere. She makes sure I'm well dressed and that the maids attend to me. She doesn't talk to me much, and when she does, she is serious, authoritarian, and firm. Never loving. She is not married. She never got married or had children. She hosts big parties in the house, and she makes me dress up and introduces me to the guests; then I go to my bedroom.

In another scene, I can't sleep. I scream. I stop talking. I get agitated, physically, my arms and legs seem to move on their own. They stretch like in a convulsion. My aunt sends me to a hospital for people who are "different." I scream at night. They are cold and aloof, except for one nurse. She is very kind and loving towards me. She comes to sit with me at the garden when it's her day off. I'm calmer, I hardly ever scream. I still wake up in the middle of the night, but most of the time I can go back to sleep after drawing. The nurse gives me colored pencils and a notebook.

Years later, I am older. I am sent to a mansion in the countryside. My Aunt Ann-Marie is there. She is old and sick. It's her home. She still doesn't talk to me much, but she is gentler than she used to be. She sits by the fire and reads or just stares at the fire, her legs covered by a soft throw. She sends for me and has me sit in the same room. She doesn't talk to me except for a few comments about the weather, or about a book, but never about my drawings. I like to draw and color. It calms me.

My aunt dies. She leaves the mansion to me. My only friend, the nurse, comes to visit sometimes. Years later, when I die, peacefully, she is there, by my side.

As our time together regressing finishes, I can't help but to speculate: "If this is not real, part of my past lives, then I have a very interesting and creative imagination."

September 15-24, 2013 – Positive Shifts at Work

It has been almost 5 months since my diagnosis of LMS, and 3 weeks since I returned from the Casa. I don't have the same drive to work. I've cut my hours considerably. I don't have the same empathy towards my patients who have been seeing me for years and still have not committed to lifestyle changes that could greatly improve their health and overall wellbeing.

I am determined to let go of patients who are chronically negative, and make no effort to change. Now, at this stage of my life, when I'm working so hard to be positive and hopeful, I get overwhelmed and pushed downwards when negative energy surrounds me.

The first two patients that morning are long timers who fit the category I just described. I ask them what they expect from me, professionally, and unless they are truly ready to put into actions changes to help themselves, I'd appreciate it if they would let go of sessions with me at this stage.

Surprisingly, they are finally ready, saying they'd appreciate a chance to continue. I share several apps, books, and websites of relaxation, empowerment, and meditation that have helped me. And so it goes for the next weeks. Not a single piece of negative feedback as I approach patients who have been resistant to changes. Hmm! Interesting.

At home, I paint two walls of my study blue, my favorite color. I donate most of my books. They have been read and just occupy space. They can be useful to others. I transform the space into my little sanctuary, where I can meditate, do yoga, relax, read.

"Intuition is a sense of knowing how to act spontaneously without needing to know why." — Sylvia Clare

FIVE MONTHS JOURNEYING WITH THE DRAGON & FULL CIRCLE WITH "THE ORIGINAL" CAT

Today is Amanda's 23rd birthday, on September 23. She is all grown up and lives in a city 2 hours away. We talk, but she isn't here for us to celebrate together.

In the evening, I'm walking with my neighbor, the one who originally told me about John of God. I tell her about my experiences in Abadiânia. When I tell her about the clairvoyant woman who told me about my son who had died, she says, "Maybe it is time to have a ceremony for him."

I walk home in the dark. On the top shelf of my closet, I find Bruno's things that I had saved for all these years. I turn the pages of the album of my pregnancy and baby shower. I read the words I wrote, including the ones when he died. I hold the clothing he wore at the hospital, as I had held him, limp body, eyes closed, without life. I remember holding his cold little fingers; the sadness felt as I said, "I will never get to see his eyes." I caress his little hat and socks. Then I reach for the little blue tin box where I kept his ashes up to 14 months ago, when I spread them at Epcot, as I had promised him when he passed (I finally let go of the ashes after the guru in Bali told me he saw my son and that I had to let him go). I can't believe my eyes. The lid of the box has a drawing of a cat walking happily on 2 feet! I laugh. In an instant, I feel that all of these cats I've been seeing are connected to this one, to Bruno, my son. I understand that this may seem odd, to say the least, but I am being true to my gut instinct.

And with this feeling of joy glowing in my heart, I turn the lights off. I realize today is another 23. I simply smile and close my eyes, thinking of my sweet angel and all the lessons I have learned recently.

"The danger of venturing into uncharted waters is not nearly as dangerous as staying on shore, waiting for your boat to come in." — Charles F. Glassman

Returning to Abadiânia and the Casa

The decision to return to Abadiânia was made mid-August, during my first stay there. I felt so much positive energy and at ease there, that I knew it was the right thing to do, to make plans for my return. I fly to São Paulo and then to Brasilia. The taxi driver is waiting for me at the airport.

October 2, 2013 – I Feel at Home

I arrive at Abadiânia at 2:00 a.m. "My" cat is at the front gate of Inn São Miguel. Since everyone is still sleeping, I head to room 15, the same one I stayed in August. I immediately feel at home, even though so much has happened since..

At 6:20 a.m., after only 3 hours of sleep, I am up and dressed in white clothing. By 6:55 a.m. I'm grabbing breakfast on the go and headed to the Casa. The street is already dotted with people wearing white. I quickly get my second time card and head to the main hall, taking a seat by the front. The routine is comfortingly familiar, as are some faces.

When my line is called, I move closer to John of God. My heart beats fast. I have written three things I want on a piece of paper. He extends his left hand, as I kneel down.

"I've returned from the United States," I say.

"How are you feeling?"

"Very well. Only insomnia is a problem."

"I want you to bring the results of your tests," he says.

I tell him it will be done in 3 weeks.

"I want to see them. Have two crystal baths."

He hands me a prescription for passiflora. I head to the next room to receive a blessing. I feel light and happy. It seems the entity wasn't worried about me, as he didn't recommend spiritual surgery, and that is good. I sit with my eyes closed, receive the blessing, and head to get the Casa soup.

I book two crystal baths. As I lie on the bed, the tension between my eyes starts again. It lasts the whole time, but I still feel relaxed.

The lunch back at the inn is great as always. I notice there are more Brazilians here this week. By 1:20 p.m. I head back to the Casa and join the current, which lasts four and a half hours. I don't see the eyes parading through my closed eyes that I have seen in the past. I also don't feel the intense heat on my hands. I feel more at ease. At night I meet some women at the inn. They're new, and I answer many of their questions.

October 3, 2013 – Back to the Casa, Feels Like Arriving Home

At 7:15 a.m. I arrive at the Casa and join everyone in the main hall. I head to the entity with my friend Chester's picture. He takes the picture and says, "This I will keep for "work." I worry. This is done when the situation is very serious.

The activities at the Casa and around it are all familiar, but something has changed. I don't analyze everything. I don't doubt, I don't add "supposedly" to every sentence describing what happens at the Casa. I immerse into the process, doing my part, and receiving peace, hope, and joy. Meditation and prayer happens effortlessly.

October 4, 2013 – Letting My Intuition Guide Me

I intended not to be part of the current this morning, but already seated in the hall, I feel an urge to lend a hand to the current. So, I stand and head to the meditation room.

In the afternoon I ask for permission to go to the waterfall, which is granted.

October 5, 2013 – Meeting Casa Veterans and Going to Waterfall

I take my meals with an Australian woman, Beata, a 37-year-old widow who has a house here, and Renata, a 33-year-old from Lithuania, who has been coming to Abadiânia for the past 4 years. She was in a coma for two and a half weeks after a car accident in Atlanta, and spent 8 months in intense rehab before she could return to her home country. She shares that she couldn't walk when she came, that now she can walk without help and is doing much better. She comes back to Abadiânia at various times and stays for 2 months.

I walk to the waterfall. It feels wonderful. I feel the cleansing. The cold water is energetic. It's interesting that I never feel cold after going under the waterfall — just so full of energy! I perform the ritual with two French women who have been here 4 times before. It never seems to stop amazing me that people from different countries return many times and report feeling better, even well.

October 6, 2013 – My Sister Andrea Arrives in Abadiânia

After breakfast, I have two crystal bath sessions. Again, pressure between my eyes, almost to the point of being painful! I still don't understand this. I know that it is the area of the third eye — intuition — but why the painful tension?

I meet a young woman from Austria. This is her second time. She has multiple sclerosis but we can't tell. She says when she came 2 years ago, her hand trembled and her eyes felt like pictures were constantly in motion, like a filmstrip. After her first time in Abadiânia, she separated from her husband of 12 years and is happier now with her two young boys.

My sister Andrea arrives around 11:30 a.m. Now things will change. Sister time!

After lunch we take a walk to the viewpoint where we can see the valley on both sides. We laugh, talk, and have a great time.

I meet another young woman from Ireland. She says she came after watching a show on TV. She suffers from depression but says that here she feels great. She plans on staying a little longer. She is finishing college and is writing a dissertation while here.

October 7, 2013 – Sister Time is Healing

We have a crystal bed after breakfast, and my sister finds it very relaxing. I still feel that strong sensation between my eyes. My sister is impressed with the number of foreigners speaking English, French, and German and also with how clean the Casa is. In the afternoon we walk to the waterfall. There are two Australian guys there. We follow the ritual, which I truly enjoy. It feels so right.

My sister shares that right before getting under the waterfall, she felt such strong energy she almost fainted. She is surprised, since she didn't have any expectations whatsoever before getting here.

We walk the dirt road up the hill to the Casa, taking time to admire the view, the trees, and the birds, feeling one with it all. It's hot. The sky is cloudy. By the time we arrive at the inn it is 6:00 p.m. and dinner is being served.

At night we watch the documentary, *Curas e Milagres* ("Healing" in English), about John of God and the Casa. My sister really enjoys it. We talk and then say good night.

I'm still not sleeping well. Actually, it has been worse here. I wake up three times per night, even with meds and meditation. I have also been doing yoga once or twice per day. I feel good during the day, with energy, but I know that the good night of sleep, which is stressed as vital at the Casa, is important for the body, mind, and spirit. I'm still hopeful that my insomnia will disappear.

It rains hard during the night, with lightning, thunder, and wind.

October 8, 2013 – Another Peaceful Day

Morning is peaceful, like most days here. I spend time at the Casa grounds under the mango trees and at the bookstore. I have another crystal bed and I feel the same pressure between my eyes. Is it ever going to go away? I visit a café. At 3:00 p.m. there's singing at the soup tables. I enjoy it, as before.

I chat with Enrique for a long time. It's amazing the stories we hear here! He has suffered a lot but seems to have found his place on Earth here, since he moved to the inn almost a year ago.

My sister attends orientation.

Marco tells me I should ask the entity for permission to be a guide since "You are already guiding people anyways." My sister agrees, but I don't know about this. I know the rhythm of the Casa, but there is just too much I still don't understand.

October 9, 2013 – "Recognized" by Entity!

I get up at 5:00 a.m., do yoga, and by 6:50 a.m. I'm getting breakfast. A large group of Canadians from Montreal and Quebec has arrived. At 7:10 a.m. we take our seats at the main hall of the Casa. I pray at the triangle. Mid-morning I go in front of the Entity, who says, before I have a chance to open my mouth, *"Eu já lhe conheço. Sente na minha corrente."* (I already know you from another life. Sit on my current room). "You have permission to bring people to the Casa, if you want."

I sit on the main current to meditate. I realize that this is the first time my heart doesn't beat fast before the entity. Later I'm told, "The Entity must have felt very good energy from you, that you're ready."

My sister is disappointed that the Entity didn't give her a chance to talk and just handed her a prescription. I explain that this isn't necessarily bad. She hears the stories we all share during ours meals and seems impressed.

During the line inside the current rooms today, the Entity tells people to open their eyes. He asks the woman with breast cancer, "Show with your fingers how big your tumor is?" She makes an oval shape the size of an egg. He asks if there is a doctor in the room. A man stands and goes to the front and examines the woman's breast. He is told to show how big the tumor is. He does so, showing a bigger tumor. The entity moves his hands around in front of the woman's breast for a while and tells the doctor to examine her again. "There is no tumor," the doctor says, amazed.

In the afternoon I sit on the main current. This time, John, an Australian man on a wheelchair calls me to sit by him. He says that

I belong there, and this is the reason I was there, and that it isn't an accident that we are both here.

He says when he saw the Entity for the first time he was told, "You must stay for three months." He has been here for four years, "Leaving only once to fix his wheelchair," he says with a big smile. The current lasts four and a half hours. It's easier than before to meditate for hours. The time passes effortlessly, somehow. At 5:00 p.m. I go for a 20-minute crystal bed session. For the first time, there is no tension between my eyes! I'm happily surprised. Today is a special day of firsts: the way the entity talked to me, moving me on to the main current, and now relaxed with no strange sensation around the third eye area. I feel happy, light.

After dinner, we retire to our rooms. I've been reading the book I received as a gift 7 or 8 years ago, *The Tibetan Book of Living and Dying*. I like it. It puts together in words what I have been slowly learning and practicing about Buddhism and, even more interesting, Spiritism and also, to a certain degree, Hinduism. Many similarities in the concepts of reincarnation; meditation/prayer; law of cause and effect; "the observer;" a person's path being determined not by fate but by his/hers own input; et cetera. Karma is also defined similarly.

October 10, 2013 – Amazing Stories

I still wake up two or three times in the night. By 6:00 a.m. I'm doing yoga. By 6:50 a.m. I'm having breakfast. My plan is to pass by the entity in the a.m. to present the photos from American friends with history of cancer and do current in the afternoon. However, when I show the pictures, the entity says I must come back with the photos in the afternoon, so, no current today. This is how things happen here: The rhythm is random, unpredictable, but it's all good in the end.

At the main hall they call in anyone who wishes to have spiritual surgery. Spontaneously, my sister asks me, "Should I go?"

"If it feels right to you, go." And she goes to the line and in.

I reflect on all that happens here: every single story we hear, and there are so many! All report feeling better physically and emotionally. Some with slow progress, like the Lithuanian girl, others with miraculous results. Angela shares that she arrived at the

Casa as a last resort. She had a tumor in her brain the size of an egg. She weighed 36 kg couldn't see or walk. Doctors gave her 40 days of life. That was 12 years ago! She moved to Abadiânia 2 years ago and she volunteers at the Casa, and is a caretaker for people who aren't able to care for themselves.

I go to a hairdresser. She doesn't go to the Casa, but she shares all the amazing cures she has witnessed. She tells about a Greek woman who had an abdominal cancer. She says the woman looked pregnant. There was no hope for her. She is still alive many years later, and her stomach is normal. She moved to Abadiânia.

And the stories go on and on. A group of 14 from Canada arrive at the inn. They have meetings and seem very intense. A large group from Sweden is arriving next week. I meet an Ethiopian woman who lives in Virginia. She is here for the fourth time in a year, with her daughter who is 4 years old. She wears traditional Ethiopian clothing and meditates often. There are small European children in wheelchairs. There are many young people from Australia, Austria, Switzerland, Germany, the United States and more

By 9:00 p.m. I'm in bed. The days are long here. I feel tired but content.

October 11, 2013 – Last Day at The Casa

Today is my last Casa-Day of this trip. I wake up early, as usual, and by 7:00 a.m. I'm in the current line. The current lasts 4 hours. With my eyes closed, I can hear the entity from time to time, "I'm going to help you see again. Take these glasses off and go sit in the current. You will see a rainbow while your eyes are closed. See what happens next."

"Have you gone to your doctor? I'm going to help this tumor disappear but you must go to the doctor. Bring me the test results."

"Go have 6 crystal baths, then have the spiritual surgery. I'm going to help you."

He tells a man in a wheelchair, "You don't need this. Stand up and walk." And so the man does.

We are instructed to drink the water offered after each current and to go have the free soup. There is a camera crew there today, filming for a documentary.

Back at the inn, my sister reports she is feeling well now. She rested all morning in bed, nauseous after the spiritual surgery. She is so surprised, as she didn't expect to feel anything. I smile and say: "And so it is here. The unexpected happens."

"Peace comes from within. Do not seek it without." — Gautama Buddha

BACK HOME AGAIN

I return home from the Casa in peace and with a rhythm within, not alienated with the pace of life and work. Little by little I clear my morning schedule so that I can have a peaceful morning routine. I get up, do yoga in my room (or just listen to one of my meditation recordings), make a green smoothie, take my passiflora with intention, and light a candle on my altar. Then I go for a short walk with Ziggy, have breakfast, and take a cup of warm coffee to my "blue room," holding it, feeling its warmth, as I stare at the candle flame. When it's time, I do guided healing meditation, Deepak Chopra being one of my favorite guides, or I just let the sound of relaxation music, or silence, permeate my being. Ziggy is always by my side, every morning. He is a blessing and a great companion.

Quiet time, before all that has happened these past months, was an alien concept to me. In my mind, it translated to laziness and guilty followed. It felt as if I couldn't afford it because there was always so much to be done. Now, downtime is my life source, and in it I find peace and strength, within the silence. I find a supreme force, self, that in the past I only found while hiking in faraway lands, villages. Now, I can take the time to just be practically anywhere, as peace is always with me, as it resides within.

"To dare is to lose one's footing momentarily. Not to dare is to lose oneself." — Soren Kierkegaard

GOING PUBLIC TO POTENTIALLY HELP OTHERS WITH LMS

Inspired by the Facebook page created by my friend Melisa to keep her family and friends updated about her treatment, I decide to create a page as well, but with a different goal. My intention is that my public page containing the word "Leiomyosarcoma" on its name can be easily found by people diagnosed with the Dragon. By posting positive news and my celebration of life and good results every 3 months, as I travel the road of recovery, others on similar journeys can potentially feel hope and in company. Whenever I searched for sites about LMS, I found only gloomy news, which made me even more scared and hopeless. I want to feel and share hope. And so *"My Journey with Dx of Leiomyosarcoma"* Facebook page is born. This is a call that excites my spirit, and even if I reach only a couple of people, my goal will be achieved.

October 20, 2013 – Time to Start Tests for 6-Month Checkup

Why does a little anxiety still manage to sneak in when it is time for the blood tests? At least I manage to help fade it away now, with breathing meditation.

October 22, 2013 – CT-Scan Day

I wake up, meditate, and take my first bottle of barium contrast. I go for a walk with Ziggy while listening to relaxing music. It's a little cool, but the beauty of the oak tree-lined road with the hanging Spanish moss seems to embrace me, soothing the uneasiness that's trying to poke in. An hour later, I'm back home for the second bottle of barium. It's always harder to swallow this one. I quickly push away thoughts of the side effects of this and the radiation of scans. Technology, including radioactivity, becomes an ally, not an enemy, once cancer has knocked on your door.

The drive to the cancer center is quiet. I keep my headphones on, listening to the positive affirmations by Louise Hay. The check-in procedure is familiar to me by now. I sit. John has already zoned out into his iPhone world, and I find a *National Geographic*. It's the magazine's all-time favorite cover: the girl from Afghanistan.

I remember some years back reading about when the magazine tracked her down. In her 30s, she looked so much older. Life didn't seem to have been kind to her: hard work, lack of hospitals/medical care. What different worlds we live in, within the same universe, I think. If she had cancer, she would not have medical help. I feel blessed.

I'm called in for the procedure. I lie on the movable table of the scanner; IV contrast is injected in a vein in my arm. I feel the warm sensation that travels through the inside of my body. This time it goes to my head as well! It scares me for a second, but I again I let go. I can't and shouldn't analyze or fear. It is as it is. I surrender.

I must find relaxation within. My headphones are on. I close my eyes and transport myself to the faraway land of Tibet once again, while minding commands to hold my breath from time to time. I go in and out of the scanner, letting it "photograph" my organs, cells, praying that no "lights" will shine, as I hope and meditate to be cancer free.

"*I am strong, I am healthy. I am cured.*" I repeat that over and over and over again, silently. Over and over again, day and night…

October 23, 2013 - Yannick's 18th Birthday

I take the day off. Amanda is here and we have breakfast together, after my meditation and morning walk. I keep repeating silently: "I am strong. I'm healthy. I'm cured." I feel very hopeful. I pray to the entities of the Casa and to my Spirit Guide, for all in need, and for myself. Yes, for myself, now without guilt or embarrassment. I take pizza to Yannick's school. It's his last year before college. I want to be and will be around for his college graduation, for Amanda's and his wedding, to hold my grandkids. I want all of these moments to be lived, so I'll be alive and I will survive The Dragon.

"Life is full of beauty. Notice it. Notice the bumblebee, the small child, and the smiling faces. Smell the rain, and feel the wind. Live your life to the fullest potential, and fight for your dreams." — Ashley Smith

CELEBRATING 6 MONTHS "DRAGON FREE"

October 24, 2013 – Tic-Tac, Tic-Tac...

The hours seem to drag on and on. I have an oncologist's appointment in the afternoon. The waiting at the office is long. I make small talk. I glance at magazine pictures. I'm a little on edge even though much better than during other appointments. I breathe deeply. I'm called in. Time passes slowly, but finally the doctor comes in, gives a smile, and says. "It's all clear."

YES! YES! YES! I can exhale again.

October 25, 2013 – End Let the Party Begin

Determined to celebrate 6 months cancer free, I invite friends for a dress-up Halloween party. I bought a costume 2 years ago, but never wore it. I just had to laugh when I find it and read its name: "Lady Luck." Yes! That's me! And so, feeling and dressing fortunate to be cancer free, I share a joyful night with friends, celebrating life.

Aunt Mil passed away the same night, at age 93. I don't feel much sadness. I now know that "the other side" exists, is part of the circle of life and death, the ones before and the ones to come. There's no way of knowing when that will be, for me. Today I am all about celebrating that I am healthy, alive, and filled with hope.

October 30, 2013 – Verbalizing the Importance of Guidance on How to be Positive

I vent to both my doctors that all physicians I have seen, including them, gave me grim news about my diagnosis, declaring the only thing I could do was to be "positive." However, not a single one pointed me in any direction. No hints, guidance, nothing at all about how to find positivity in the emotional chaos I was thrown into. I share that it took two lonely, frightful, teary months for me to start finding light on my own and in the most unexpected ways.

Friends and family aren't with you at all times of the day and night: you are alone when the tears seem endless, when the sorrow is so painful that it's hard to breathe, when the grief cuts through your core, when you long for the freedom to feel healthy, and when you are introduced to death, and somehow you befriend it. Death is an enemy that can take away all you hold true to your heart, but yet, it is inevitable. Understanding and accepting it as an ally, is a must.

Celebrating 6 months Dragon free, and also Halloween, as *Lady Luck*.

"I believe in God, but not as one thing, not as an old man in the sky. I believe that what people call God is something in all of us. I believe that what Jesus and Mohammed and Buddha and all the rest said was right. It's just that the translations have gone wrong." — John Lennon

EMBRACING MY SPIRITUAL GROWTH

Since the day I re-discovered Dr. Weiss, many enlightened beings have come into my life to be by my side, to help me move through the grief, to understand that this journey and all others, are but one, and that the destinations are the continuum of rolling stops, where we let go of unwanted, unfulfilling luggage, and move in search of meaningful ones: *Love, compassion, kindness, harmony.*

Dr. Weiss, Dr. Chopra, Dr. Wayne Dyer, Louise Hay, volunteers at the Casa, the entities of the Casa, sons of the Casa, and some special friends, each has taught me how to find positivity, which can be translated to hope, love, and fulfillment, within my diagnosis of cancer and my journey with The Dragon.

My diagnosis no longer represents a proclamation of my upcoming death. Right now it represents a pit stop, or better yet, a detour in my life, a side-journey that was at first bleak, dark, cold, solitary, and depleted of any light. Well, this station, or detour, is getting lighter, warmer, more cheerful, and filled with possibilities, since generous souls have guided me to see the hidden lessons to be learned and messages to be seen. Step by step, stone by stone, I'm starting to pave a new path that is taking me (and hopefully others) from where I was, to where I simply am, now, in this moment that I have.

As for what is to come, I still have a lot to learn about trying not to predict it, not to anticipate it, not to dwell on it. I learn each day about the power of intention, of believing with my heart and soul, and not my mind. My left side brain peeks in quite often, but I'm learning to observe it, let its thoughts go, and fade away.

I have been taking "virtual courses" in positivity with the help of my iPhone apps, my YouTube teachers, and writers. A master positivity teacher also lives in the depth of my heart and soul; I just need to dig it out to the surface.

I have been going again to the Tibetan meditation center every Sunday. I feel at home there. I'm learning more about Buddhism and about life, death, and reincarnation, little by little.

Since I turned my home office into my blue meditation room, I've learned to find peace and quiet at home as well. My walls are blue, just like were the ones in my room when I was a teenager in Brazil, and like the infinite sky in a glorious spring day. I've gathered all my Buddha statues from the Himalayas, my 3 Saint Francis of Assisi, my Indian Ganesh, my Russian St. Mary, my Brazilian candomblé deity, a beautiful Tibetan incense box, and candles, all under my colorful Tibetan Thangka of Chenrezik and the Triangle from the Casa, which hang on the blue wall. This is a room where I can go within and can just be. I feel grateful for this space I call my own and for all I have.

I've donated most of my books, finding that it's time to share with others who can enjoy them. Every morning and evening I light a candle or two, I say prayers, and I sit in silence, incense burning, meditating in stillness. No guilt, no feeling lazy. I've learned to allow myself to just be. Now I have a greater understanding of the monks I observed throughout the Himalaya. Now I understand the importance of connecting to the self and to all that there is.

*"And when you want something, all the universe
conspires in helping you to achieve it."*
— Paulo Coelho

THE TRAVELER WITHIN & THE SINKHOLES

And then November arrives. I go to a party, bringing a puppy as a gift for a friend. It was so uplifting! Then I chatted, played Ping-Pong, felt cheerful and healthy. Cancer is far away from my mind in days like this one. Dragon who?

As the days pass, the traveller within me resurfaces. It takes me back in time, to the present, and into the future, in just a fraction of a moment. The dialogues are endless, fulfilling, open, unleashed, and often deep to the core.

The trails of San Felasco Park become my sacred place in nature. The statuesque pine trees and the mysterious oak trees with hanging Spanish moss become the silent witnesses of my soul. As my feet, mind, and heart step on the ground covered by orange and yellow leaves, I see, hear, and smell autumn; but deep inside, I feel the colors of spring. I feel free, healthy, and happy with my own companion.

While immersed in peace and joy, feeling one with nature, cancer is non-existent. I feel alive, peaceful, light. I breathe serenity. I feel love. I feel whole, and connected.

I see the sinkholes present on the trails as a metaphor of the uncertainty of it all, brought and introduced to me by The Dragon. The ground gets swallowed, without warning, changing the landscape forever. But the terrain eventually settles down, inviting new plants, new life, and restored beauty. Chaos vanishes; calmness reappears.

And so it is with the cancer. The Dragon appeared out of nowhere, sucking down my "landscape," taking me below the ground, without footing. But, just like with the sinkholes, I feel slowly covered with lushness, my body and mind restoring, re-shaping, and being transformed. From the ugliness of the mystery of leiomyosarcoma, a new me is emerging, growing and flourishing, somehow.

Had it not been for the diagnosis, which allowed me to give myself permission to take time off without feeling lazy or guilty, I wouldn't be in the woods merging with nature, answering to the invitations of the traveller within to walk the trails here, while reliving the memories of the ones traveled before.

November 17, 2013 – Serendipity and The Aleph

Paulo Coelho is a Brazilian author well known all around the world. However, I admit, with shame, that I never read any of his books, although I have intended to for a very long time.

While at the Miracles Happen workshop with Dr. Weiss, I thought I heard him say Paulo Coelho's name, with a heavy accent, of course, followed by the quote "Life is the train, not the station." Hum! Did I hear it correctly? Did he quote the Brazilian author? I realized I didn't even know what Coelho wrote about, and decided that I was finally going to purchase and read some of his work. But this was last July, the months have passed, and today, I still haven't read any of his books.

It is now a sunny Saturday morning in November. Over a super sweet cup of Cuban coffee, intention to go to the farmer's market diverted, I find the words slipping out of my mouth, chatting with a person I barely know. The hours pass without us noticing it, the coffee got cold, and surprisingly, I am sharing all that has happened to me over the past months, without filtering what I still find bizarre and can't explain. I am holding nothing back, revealing my experiences, from Dr. Weiss's workshop to regressions, and even John of God. That's when I hear: "It sounds like the book *Aleph*, by Paulo Coelho. Have you read it?" "No," I shamefully admit, "I haven't read any of his books actually."

I haven't disclosed my experiences to many, and here I am, comfortably sharing them to a semi-stranger, somehow without worry about being judged. A connection is made, and a beautiful friendship is born.

In a few hours, a copy of *Aleph* was on my hands. I started to read it and I could not put it down. It explores the experiences of the author with past life regressions among other things. I feel less freakish, I must confess, knowing that a famous author believes in regression too. I realize we both have wandered some of the same corners of the world, with similar longings, discoveries, and anguish. He is a pilgrim of the world, and so am I. He has set off on long-dreamed adventures, and so have I. But there was more, much more. So many of his words touched me, seemed to have been written for me, at his moment of crisis in my life, of cancer. "What hurts us is what heals us." "The present moment is where all signs, parallel worlds, and miracles are to be found. Time doesn't really exist." "Tears are the blood of the soul."

I kept reading and was astonished to recognize the quote shared by Dr. Weiss at the workshop: "*Life is the train not the station.*" I understand its meaning. I reflect on it.

I turn off the lights, but a quote stays with me: "*Dreamers can't be tamed.*" Hum! I can relate to that. I dare to dream again, to bet on the unimaginable.

November 23, 2013 – Discovering a Magical Little Place

It's another 23rd, and keeping up with my new tradition, I plan to do something fun and special. The plan was to go zip lining, but I came up with a cold. So, I settle for a drive to a roadside pizza place in a historical small town. It's a bright sunny day and sitting outdoors under an old oak tree was delightful.

Looking for a place to have a coffee, Moosewood was discovered. It is a quaint little coffee shop in a cracker style house. I fell in love with the place immediately, and over the next months, many sweet memories of quiet time on the porch, at times watching the sunset over a delicious pastry and a warm cup of coffee, were born.

I stop to thank the Universe for my increasing understanding of "it" all and how everything seems to be connected in time and space. Regressions are starting to make sense. Reincarnation is starting to make sense. I breathe what feels like love; my heart beats as knowing, and in appreciation of life, of these moments. I feel pure affection for the amazing people who have stepped into my journey, effortlessly, and I reflect on the quote: *"If you want to see a rainbow, you have to learn to like the rain."* My current *"rain"* is this journey with The Dragon, but I'm starting to see *"rainbows"* in my life.

Back in my blue room, I delight myself with the memories of this day. I had witnessed the sky display several periods of daylight, and into the night, from *the* porch.

"If we seek something, that same thing is seeking us," said Coelho on *Aleph!*

I allow my authenticity to bloom and I get a glimpse of pure bliss. A day to be treasured.

*"Perhaps death doesn't mean goodbye, but rather,
'til we meet again."* — Paul Stefaniak

THANKSGIVING AND BRUNO'S 25

On Thanksgiving night, 1988, I had been in labor for two days when I delivered my already deceased 8-month baby boy. Today Bruno would be 25 years old.

For the past few weeks I had been planning to plant a garden in his honor outside the window of the blue room. I would be able to see it from my blue daybed. I have bought a baby Buddha statue, a gardenia, some snapdragons (Ha! Didn't realize they have the word dragon until now!), and a dragon fruit (I purchased it because I love the fruit and it reminds me of Bali); I plan on getting a climbing rose bush too.

Thanksgiving morning came, and I had not planted the little garden yet. As I enter the meditation room after breakfast, still in my PJs, I decided to venture out in the cold. I moved the Buddha statue and started to plant the flowers. Once finished, I called the family to the blue room, and pointing to the garden, with tears in my eyes, I said: "I know you don't remember, but Bruno would be 25 years old today. In his memory, I am creating a small garden." The kids hugged me; John kept quiet and walked away.

In the afternoon, we go to the Parker's home to celebrate the day with friends. I feel thankful for the peace and hope I have found, despite the craziness of the past months.

November 26, 2013 - Experiencing The Aleph?

But what is aleph? "The place beyond time and space; the beginning and the end." Coelho wrote: "Love is beyond time, or rather, love is both time and space, but focused on one single constantly evolving point, The Aleph."

I find myself having a cup of coffee among trinkets at a little antique store. Dreaming, I feel these most beautiful eyes piercing mine, over and over again. "Am I experiencing the aleph?" I wander.

November 27, 2013 - Preparing for an Early Christmas

Christmas tree goes up to the mystical sound of Deva Premal, as a friend suggested. I loved the vibe it created. I rejoice.

I get a message, "Any obstacle or challenge can be faced. People's mindset keeps them from growing and advancing." I answer, "Where is the courage?" "Inside you."

I know that's the truth. I just have to dig it out.

November 29, 2013 - More Unusual Happenings I Don't Even Try to Explain

The day after Thanksgiving, I write the following email to Sylvia, the Canadian Clairvoyant I met in Abadiânia 3 months ago.

Dear Sylvia

Yesterday it was Thanksgiving. It was also Bruno's 25th birthday. Twenty-five years ago, it had been a week since I dreamed of a little bright light coming out of me, and he passed. The doctor advised that I keep him inside me, still, already with his soul gone, until I'd go into labor. A week after he passed, I delivered his little 8-month perfect body, on Thanksgiving night. I held him, I cried, I said good-bye, but he never left my heart and soul. Thank you for coming to help him ascend. I am forever grateful to you and God, for showing me what I still don't understand, but chose to embrace.

With my deepest love, Patricia

November 30, 2013 – Unexpected and Surreal Response

Dear Patricia

Thank you for the most heart-warming e-mail! As I was reading the e-mail, my Spirit Guides and Bruno related a message in your honor. This is the message:

"There is a special place in the Kingdom of God (in the Spirit World). It is called 'God's Garden of the Rose'. A mother's love is a precious vibration in the Universe. And is a vibration that has a multi-purpose beauty. Patricia - Your constant concern and love for Bruno has made it possible for both God and Bruno to utilize those specific vibrations of love. It is the magic of God's rose (God's love) that binds the 2 worlds together.

Bruno is standing beside me with a magnificent bouquet of white gardenias and a message for his incredible mother. The gardenias are infused with the God's Light. Gardenias represent Secret Love (the love you held in your heart for these 25 years), Refinement of Spirituality (your developing relationship with God) and Purity of Heart.

Bruno is presently working as a gardener greeting children as they transition into the Spirit World. Bruno has a special gift for working with children on the other side, due to the Spiritual love he felt while in your womb!

Spiritual Blessing for a Merry Christmas and Happy New Year. Warren for Sylvia

In disbelief, I answer immediately:

Oh my God Sylvia.

Thank you so very much. You will not believe it, but yesterday I started to plant a little garden to celebrate Bruno. It is a little spot right outside my meditation and room. I planted a gardenia, which has my very favorite scent in any garden. My grandfather had a gardenia in his yard. I love its smell. It takes me back in time.

As for <u>roses</u>, I absolutely love them too. I had planned on planting one at Bruno's garden. Once I planted the first plants, I called the family and showed the garden to them, as tears rolled down. So, we both share a love for children and gardens!!

I hope you are in good health and that you enjoy a long peaceful and happy life. You are an angel. Big hug for you and Warren, with the scent of gardenias.

Patricia (and Ziggy)

December 1, 2013 – More!!!!

Mind that Sylvia and I only emailed each other once, back in October when I wrote saying I was back in Abadiânia. She never heard details of how Bruno died or any specifics about my life. Now she writes again:

Dear Patricia

Just before my meditation this morning, I decided to take another look at the photo of the garden in memory of Bruno you sent. When I held the photo in my hand, Bruno came with this message:

"If my father is experiencing any discomfort in his right leg or right side, with loving concern, Bruno suggests he makes an appointment to see a doctor.

Please do not be alarmed with this message. Many times messages from the Spirit World prevent further complications due to their ability to see into the future.

Bruno also showed me a red address book. Does this have any meaning for you?

December 4, 2013 – Intrigued

It took me a few days to answer Sylvia. I couldn't find any red address book and sharing the email with John didn't go that well, so I didn't know how to tell her. But, today I am ready to write what was the truth:

111

Dear Sylvia and Warren

After receiving your last message, I called my children and John. I started by saying that "I can't explain how things happen, but I choose to believe them." Then I asked Amanda: "What is my favorite flower?" She answered "gardenias, like in your grandpa garden, right?" Then I asked: "What is my other favorite flower?" She answered: "Roses." I proceeded to read aloud the messages we have exchanged. Tears rolled down my face as I read the messages from Bruno.

Amanda was impressed and said. "Wow. This is really interesting!" Yannick said: "That's amazing! How can she communicate with the dead?" John didn't even take his eyes off his computer screen!!!

The kids asked if he had been feeling any pain. He said, "No." I reminded him that his lower back started to hurt 10 days ago and he could hardly walk. He says that it was nothing and he is okay now. I just said: "Message delivered."

It has been uneasy for me that he is not "in touch" with the new deepening of my spiritually. I've been spending more time in my meditation room with Ziggy, my puppy (which Bruno says he wanted me to adopt, as you told me, without knowing I had a puppy). I fear that we will grow more and more distant; as we don't share the same beliefs, spirituality, and passions. I need companionship.

Sorry but I do not have a red address book. I have only a pink and a blue one.

On the 21st we leave to Bali. I will meet the guru who saw Bruno and told me I had to let him go, back in May 2012. He did not know my story or me at all, just like you. I was so shocked and didn't understand what he meant by "letting go", until you saw Bruno and conveyed his messages, in Abadiânia. (The guru also said I had something wrong in my stomach, but I denied it. He said, "yes you do, you just don't know it yet." A couple of months later I started to bleed more heavily, and 6 months later the tumor was found, in my uterus!!!)

With a hug in your hearts and prayers for health and happiness, Patricia

December 19, 2013 – A Red Address Book!

I write another email, again in disbelief:

Dear Sylvia

As I said, I don't have a red address book. However, yesterday at 5am, I got up to look for a card to write a note to a special and supportive friend. I then saw this stationary box I was given as a gift about 10 years ago, with a jungle picture motif. We both love Africa, I quickly thought, then preceded to open it. I have rarely used anything from this stationary box. When I opened it, the first thing to catch my eyes was an address book. In RED letters, it said on the cover: "Red Address Book." Could this be it? What Bruno was referring to as the Red address book? If so, what would be the meaning?

December 20, 2013 – Hmm!

Dearest Patricia

Thank you for taking the time out of your busy holiday season to respond to the matter relating to the red address book. I believe in my heart and Bruno is saying, that the address book is verification from him that he is constantly maintaining a Spiritual watch over his beloved Mother. Bruno is sharing that it was important for you to open the box and find the address book when you were looking for the card. Sometimes we do not understand Spirit guidance or Spirit information. Bruno says that from time to time addresses and phone numbers change in people's lives, and Bruno accepts the change in circumstances.

Bruno is attracted to my vibrations, as I too lost a child many years ago. He is saying that there is a situation that occurred 10 years ago that he would like you to recall (very close to the time that you received the address book). Sylvia and Warren

Are these flukes? Coincidences? At this point, with all that has happened along my journey, I just don't think so anymore. What are they then? Who am I to know?

"To dare is to lose one's footing momentarily. Not to dare is to lose oneself." — Soren Kierkegaard

FINALLY READY TO LISTEN AND RESPECT MY DEEPEST DESIRES

I just realized that I didn't journal much during November and December. I spent hours and hours at cafes, hiking, reading, chatting and laughing, besides meditating. Now I find myself verbalizing more, instead of writing, my thoughts, desires, and fears. I share the love I feel within me. I feel more alive and hopeful. I feel that I deserve to give love and receive love, and to find true companionship. I feel empowered to go the distance to find what I long for, as I believe I deserve it. Yes, maybe for the first time in my life, I am truly ready to put my needs first. I dare to proclaim "THIS IS MY TIME," my turn to be my true self and to honor my beliefs and wishes. I deserve to have, in this lifetime, what fulfills my heart and soul. It is time to let go of patterns of behavior that aren't in the best interest of my happiness. I don't know how many years I have left, but whatever amount of time I have, I don't intend to ignore what makes my heart sing. I deserve companionship and bliss.

A passage from *Aleph* says: *"Each time we embrace someone warmly, we gain an extra day of life."* I want many, many extra days in my life, to hold, to be held, and so much more. You will see Dragon. You will see.

December 5, 2013 – A Special Picnic and Hike

The day is gorgeous! The camellias are in bloom. Perfect day for a picnic and then a hike. And so I go to the trails nearby. Along the way, I spot a sinkhole filled with water covered with green algae. It looks mysterious, but the big log across it looks so inviting; the perfect place to sit and just be.

Stepping back on firm ground, I walk, until the Universe surprises me, pouring down electrifying energy, intense connectedness, magic. I feel bliss, ecstasy, and then, I keep on walking.

Leaving behind the camellias to be enjoyed by others, and as a mark of an enchanted day, I say goodbye to the trail I have grown to love, grateful for today.

December 6, 2013 – A Day of Great Surprises

I met with Jen for lunch at Cymplify. Over vegan nachos, she says that she read my diary and believes that it "is" a book. "What? A book?" I ask in disbelief. "Yes. You can publish it and help other people with diagnosis of cancer and other illnesses."

This was so unexpected. I feel joy and a little apprehension simultaneously. My intention was to publish a travel photo book about my wanderings throughout the Himalayans, Africa, India, Bali, Vietnam, Laos, and Cambodia. I am not a writer and exposing all I have gone through this year seems uncomfortable and intimidating, but the thought of helping others is magnificent. I say I will consider it.

Later in the day, with excitement, I share the news over dinner at an Indian restaurant, and the night ended with unexpected and delightful connection and hope.

Today, I chose to ignite and cultivate my passion for life, to surrender to my wishes, and to dare.

December 13, 2013 – Thoughtful Gifts

I receive a very pretty crystal candleholder from a friend. What a special gift to be treasured! I also receive the book *The Alchemist*. It seems like Christmas arrived early this year, and that is nice. Today, I celebrate life, love, and friendship.

December 16, 2013 – Awakening

I am learning to quiet down enough to hear my own soul and that of the Universe. When on a trail, sitting on a log above still water, or when watching the smoke of incense morph into assorted forms, as dancing with the morning light, I can hear the silence within. I taste peace, I smell calm. I'm slowly beginning to be still, to just be – That's awakening to *what is, and always will be.*

"Happiness is when what you think, what you say, and what you do are in harmony" —Mahatma Gandhi

AND TO BALI I GO AGAIN

It was my plan to return to Bali in March 2013, to see Komang, the boy with Harlequin ichythiosis I have been helping with medical treatment. However, my hysterectomy got in the way. I changed the date to May 2013, one year since I actually went to Bali to meet him, but the Leiomyosarcoma diagnosis got in the way.

I remember asking my oncologist during my first appointment: "Am I going to be able to travel to developing countries again, to meet sick children?"

He answered, "Yes, you are."

I added: "Isn't it dangerous as the cancer might come back in my lungs and poor countries have tuberculosis?"

He answered: "Don't worry about that."

But during those first few months I did worry and I couldn't even dream of going anywhere. I just wanted to crawl into my bed, roll up into a ball, eyes and ears closed, and simply let the tears roll down as they wished. If my body wouldn't prevent me from traveling three months post-surgery, my state of sadness sure would. The Dragon had robbed me of my livelihood, my drive to explore the unknown, to go the distance, and to find and learn about new cultures. I still thought of the ill and impoverished children to be found, but where did the courage to go, to dream, and to dare go? "How do I get out of this fearful state?" I thought then.

But life kept moving on, without stopping to feel sorry for me, and I didn't want to feel pity for myself either. The miracle started to happen when, little by little, ever so softly; I started to come out of the dark space. Then I started to create and open new doors, and I could see some light of hope shining slowly in... and so the tickets for Christmas in Bali were bought.

The flight is very long, with plenty of time to reflect on many aspects of my life and happenings of 2013. I find myself thinking about how my family is coping with my diagnosis. Each one is dealing with it in his/her own way. My husband, in denial, finds it hard to understand and respond to my emotional needs. He is respectful of my choices in relation to spirituality, but will not even consider embarking on the journey of discovery I have undertaken. Discussion about life and death is off the table. He says this is his way of protecting himself. Let's leave it at that.

My son has been surprisingly open to my spiritual quest, to ponder the questions of life, the universe, and even death, when one is confronted with the reality of life and death. He has been supportive and is coming to Bali with an open heart.

My daughter's reaction has been mixed. Deep in her heart she is supportive and probably afraid, but without realizing it, she may be in some denial too, as a way to protect herself. That worries me. She will at times display openness to my spiritual quest, but she keeps a safe distance and appears to moves on with life as if there aren't pending concerns. I am not really sure if this is the healthy way to cope, but I hope it is. I am not certain I am interpreting her feelings correctly either. It is so hard on both of us, I am sure. At times I am scared The Dragon is hurting them as much as me, and that it may take me away from them.

I check in with both kids from time to time, to make sure they are okay, and they always say "yes," adding also that they are confident I will be okay. I just love my kids so much and how I wish I could spare them of the hardship it is to witness a parent with cancer.

December 23, 2013 – A Day in Bangkok

Amanda and John are working, and I take Yannick out to get a taste of Bangkok and of Thai culture. I have been here before, so I have been to the must-see sights. We visit the exquisite Royal Palace, take a boat tour, and walk the streets, stopping at the political protest area.

At night we have dinner at Cabbage and Condoms restaurant, which has its proceeds donated to education for women to prevent pregnancy and AIDS. A good cause to support and delicious food make a great combination.

December 24 to January 4, 2014 – Family Time in Bali

The kids have been very excited about going to Bali. They have heard my Balinese tales from the trip in 2012. They are open to not letting the traffic and the potholes on the sidewalks of Ubud spoil all the wonders around us and to appreciating a taste of Balinese culture. The vibe outside the chaos of the main roads is serene, and we tasted it.

We have a very fun and diverse time in Bali, starting with Christmas at friends' home. Instead of a turkey, a whole suckling pig stuffed with fresh herbs was the centerpiece of the celebration. It was a certainly different but welcoming Christmas.

On New Years, we participated on a Black Moon Ceremony at Tony's compound. (He is the guru I met in 2012). My son got a chance to talk to him privately and was impressed, stating, "Everything he said was true!"

Memories were created as we engaged in various fun activities, from snorkeling, biking, eating Balinese delights, getting massages, monkeying around at Monkey Forest, to just taking it easy, treasuring our time together.

They got a glimpse of the Balinese essence I already knew. Flower-petal offerings everywhere, which never fails to bring serenity and a sense of peaceful joy; The soft and genuine friendliness of the Balinese people, including of the friends I'm blessed to have here; the poverty that prevails outside the resorts, spas, and restaurants which cater to tourists, as they saw at the village where we visited Komang, the little boy I have been helping for the past 2 years.

Me happy in Bali, relaxing, and getting more spiritual and physical strength.

*"The simple things are also the most extraordinary things,
and only the wise can see them."* — Paulo Coelho

FEEDING MY BODY AND SOUL IN BALI

The family has returned home. Now it is my time to focus on strengthening my body and feeding my soul. I knew coming here would help me to create a stronger body and mind connection, deepening my spirituality. I am grateful for the opportunity to care for my healing body and mind, here in this spiritual island.

I dive into the holistic vibe of Ubud, which is sure to do me good. I am attracted to the slow pace of Balinese life; I am delighted when observing the aromatic and colorful rituals that happen several times per day, on the side-walks, temples, or just about anywhere here in Ubud. The sweet smell of incense, the beautiful and delicate flower offerings, the flickering candles, and the gentle hand gestures made as silent prayers are said, seem to cast a spell on me. They relax my being and make me smile within.

Finding the Yoga Barn was vital in opening myself wider, not just to numerous types of yoga, but to various forms of meditation (Tibetan bowl meditation, Yin meditation, and more.) Each practice offers a subtle way of healing, of connecting to my deep self, and getting grounded in the present moment. The amazing thing is that although I am aware that I am fortunate to have the ability to be here, to emerge fully in all that the place has to offer, most people can have access to yoga and meditation practices at their own community and home. The Internet is filled with free guidance. Yoga and meditation are for anyone who wishes to soothe the body and the soul, making oneself stronger physically and emotionally. Thus, they provide great support for people dealing with the stress of cancer, and their loved ones too.

I have been vegetarian for many years, but since my diagnosis I have been even more health conscious. Yeah, I realize that the focus on health should always be there, but there is no way around it: once you get a serious diagnosis, particularly one for which the doctors say the only thing you can do is to be positive, you start to search for minute positive changes you can make, and nutrition is on the forefront.

At home, I make green shakes every morning. I eat more nuts, beans, and whole grains, and I choose organic products. Here in Bali, I order vegetarian Balinese food with a mixed fruit juice or lassi. It's always a complete meal, filled with fresh and nutritious ingredients (and I have never paid more than $4 per complete meal).

January 6, 2014: Living Ubud and The Alchemist

Today starts like the others this week. I wake to the sound of birds, particularly the doves that seem to call me not to miss the glory of another morning. But there is something special this morning: I am having breakfast while reading *The Alchemist* by Paulo Coelho, a gift from a dear friend. We exchange texts, and as planned, we are starting to read the book simultaneously. This simple act makes me content, feeling our connection, even if we are far and apart, and in different continents. The joy of friendship overtakes me; my heart smiles as it experience simple bliss. *"It's the possibility of having a dream come true that makes life interesting."* The Alchemist.

Early afternoon, I walk in the rain. It pours hard as I search for a place to grab lunch. The sidewalks here should have another name, one describing their uniqueness. They are dangerous, extraordinarily uneven, with tons of potholes, like I have never seen anywhere else in the world. Add rain to that, and disaster can occur at any step.

After a ginger, lemon, and honey tea at The Kafe, I climb the stairs of the Yoga Barn for another challenging 90-minute yoga class; this time advanced Vinyasa Flow. It's about 86 degrees, with humidity that feels like 100%. I've never sweated so much in my life, but, the important thing is that I feel amazing. Gently controlling my body, I let go of all thoughts. I practice just being in the moment, body, mind, and spirit in pure harmony. I feel light as I leave, and find myself talking to the instructor, Carlos, for a bit.

A new friend is waiting for me outside to snap a couple of photos, and then we sit at a café for a cooling mango, passion fruit, and ginger smoothie. Heavenly, just like Bali.

January 7, 2014: New Rhythm of Life

I've established a healthy and fulfilling routine for my days in Ubud, which include three wholesome meals, reading/relaxing time, one or two yoga classes, meditation session, walks, and a massage at a day spa. I feel healthy and at ease. I am overflowing with bliss and gratitude.

I have had dinner, a couple of times, with my Balinese friends. Today I meet Tony. Seating on the pillows on the floor, we enjoy a delicious meal. The dishes ordered seem tastier, and the conversation has a deeper tone.

*"We don't meet people by coincidence. They are meant
to cross our path for a reason."* — Unknown

A CASE OF COINCIDENCE, CHANNELING
OR SYNCHRONICITY?

While at the pool yesterday, a Scandinavian woman and her
daughter, named Amanda, like mine, recommended a small day-spa
near the hotel, as a great place to have a massage. I had passed by Jaen
Spa several times, but never felt inclined to enter.

Today, however, as I finished a meditation session, I was both
hungry and dying for a massage. It was getting late, so I headed to
Jaen Spa, without a reservation.

A young pregnant woman helps me, and I explain that I'd love
a massage, but also still need to grab dinner, and asked if she could
fit me in. She said that I can get a massage in a few minutes, and
could have my meal after. She asked where I was from, and when I
answered from the United States, she turns to the man seated on the
waiting area, saying that he was from the United States too. I couldn't
tell by his looks, since he was of Asian descent. He asks where I live
in the US, and I say Gainesville, Florida. He smiles in contentment,
saying he is from Tampa, a city near mine. Wow! The first American
I see in Bali, and he lives near where I come from. Interesting!

When I finish getting the one-hour and divine massage, the spa
is about to close, and only the pregnant woman and a young man
are there. As I pay, she asks: "What do you do?" "For a living?" I ask.
"Yes", she answers.

"I am a dietician, a nutritionist," I reply.

"Ah. Can I ask you a question? Maybe you can help me."

The young man, who I now know is her husband, starts to talk to her in Balinese. They go back and forth, and although I don't understand a word they are saying, I have the feeling he is trying to convince her not to ask me the question.

She goes on: "Is there anything I can eat or take to help with my pregnancy?"

"Are you vegetarian? Do you consume dairy products?" I ask, thinking she is probably concerned about not getting enough protein, iron, and calcium. She answers that she is vegetarian and doesn't have any dairy in her diet.

"Do you take calcium and iron supplements?" I ask, and she replies "No."

I explain the importance of taking the supplements.

She than asks me if I could sit down for a little and says she will order a vegetarian meal for the three of us. The husband appears uneasy. I find this a little strange but I sense that she needs my help, somehow; I said I could stay for a bit but there was no need to order food. She insisted, makes a phone call to a restaurant, I guess, and proceeds to close the front door.

I sat and she goes on. "I have a problem with my pregnancy. The doctor just told us the baby has a heart defect, and he needs an operation while in my womb, or he will die. The surgery has to be performed in Thailand or Singapore because this is the first case in Bali and the doctors here can't operate me." I felt so sad for her but also puzzled: Why is she telling me all of this? How can I possibly help?

She continues asking me, "Can you help me?" I don't know if she is asking for financial help or what. I say that I am very sorry and that I am just a dietician, not a doctor. The husband than says, "I told you," looking at her.

The woman vents, as she cries, that she feels alone because the only person who knows about this is her husband, and he doesn't understand, and nobody understands what she is going through. She adds that her father died young, her mother didn't want her, she was verbally abused and beaten up by the family members who took her in, and that she was treated like a dog. She was rescued from that life by her husband, who is her best friend, but now he can't help her. He doesn't know the pain she is feeling.

I feel her pain, loneliness and fear. Not knowing what to do, I felt that somehow I needed to share my own story, so she would feel that someone really understood what she was going through. Hesitantly at first, I followed my gut instinct, and say, "I understand how you feel. I have been diagnosed with cancer, a rare one without a certain treatment, and there isn't much I can do." They both say how sorry they are to hear this.

Deep inside, I feel the strongest urge to share what happened to my baby, but I'd have to tell that he died. I dwell deep inside, but my intuition spoke loud and clear: "Go on. It will help her." Still a little reluctantly, I start to talk, "I know how you feel in relation to your unborn child as well. I lost a baby in my womb when I was 8 months pregnant." Her expression changed, sadness was stamped on her face, but I could also sense that a connection, a bond, had been instantly created, that she didn't feel as alone anymore.

The dinner arrives and the conversation goes on for another couple of hours. I find myself counseling them about what to ask the doctor, how to be sympathetic to each other's needs and feelings, and more. It was 11:00 p.m. when I get up to leave, receiving strong hugs from both, and a sincere thanks.

I walk to my bungalow with sorrow in my heart, but also with a feeling of contentment. As unexpected and strange as the encounter was, I know that it happened for a reason. I know I helped them. My mind can't help but to ponder: "Was this a case of synchronicity? Channeling? Why did the woman decide to take a chance to talk to me, a complete stranger, from the hundreds of clients who go in and out of her spa? Somehow she picked me, a woman who had lost a baby and who could empathize with her." Hmm!!! This was no coincidence. I know that for sure.

January 9, 2014: Uneasiness Happens Even in Paradise

After breakfast I sit by the pool and call my sister Andrea in Brazil. We chat for a long time. Not all subjects are light. I share some insights about upcoming changes in my life. We usually find something cheerful to discuss, but this time we really have to search, as we both have heavy stuff in our minds.

I try to write, but the MacBook keeps alerting me that it is not happy. It erased my Word file yesterday, wiping out days of editing I had worked on. Instead of feeling furious, I took VERY deep and slow breaths, and convinced myself it was meant to be; I let it go.

"Forget about editing the past and concentrate on writing about Bali, the now," I told myself. Coincidently, my editor emailed me exactly the same advice!

I get a disturbing message from a dear friend. I find my heart perturbed. I try to brush it off, but it hurts me.

Early evening at a line at Yoga Barn, I briefly meet a very nice couple. We exchange a few words and say goodbye, as we headed out for a quick bite before the evening event. They take their bikes; I walk. Surprise, surprise! We end up at the same restaurant, sharing a great meal and chat. It felt as one of those instant connections.

Sound healing with Tibetan ancient bowls is magical. Meditative state is easier to attain. I heal as I relax. I let go and rejoice.

Although I go to sleep with my body relaxed, my mind wanders, as there is uneasiness deep within. I was wrongly judged earlier in the day, and that left an underlying subtle hurt that has kept insisting on lingering. There's an urge to justify myself for the harsh judgment I received, particularly because it came from someone I care deeply about. I'm sad and I decided to write an email.

At 2:00 a.m., I am awake. I get my computer out to write to my daughter, sending her a link to Louise Hay's *I Can Do It* book reading, as I promised. I turn the computer and lights off and close my eyes. The frogs go on making mating sounds. It takes a while, but I eventually fall asleep, just to find myself awake again at 4:00 a.m.

I don't want to write. I want nothing else but to sleep. Insomnia bothers me, as it has always done. Yoga, meditation, walks, writing, eating well — what else does my mind need to just rest itself and my body? What else? No caffeine, no alcohol, dark room, going within. Nothing seems to work. I make a decision to take a Xanax and just let it put me down. That keeps me asleep for 3 hours. "That was it?" I scream inside. And to make matters worse, I wake up uneasy, now feeling down. I don't want to get up out of bed even though I hear the sounds of the dove calling me, as the sunlight peaks through the drapes on the windows.

So, here I am, writing, trying to purge the uneasiness, snap out of sadness. I am in Bali, for crying out loud, to restore myself and for deeper healing. "Snap out of it, woman," part of me says. But the other part just wants to crawl into a ball and not hear the sounds of the new day. As I finish writing this entry, I already feel better, enough to plant my feet on the ground, determined to get going. Now I will turn off the computer, light an incense stick, say a prayer, and greet the new day. And so I go, venturing into a new day.

January 10, 2014 – Meaningful Ties are Created

After breakfast I read a little and go for a delightful walk by a rice paddy. It feels like an effortless meditation, binding with nature, breathing the fresh air, watching the birds gliding above the bright lime-green fields.

On my way back, someone calling my name out loud surprises me. I turn to see Nina and Russ on their bikes, the couple I met yesterday. They say they have been looking for me, as they made this healthy drink with fermented dragon fruit among other things. They hand me a big bottle filled with a deep fuchsia colored juice.

Heading to the hotel, passing in front of the little Jaen Spa, Putu, the owner, runs outside calling my name with open arms, giving me a big hug. She had just returned from her husband's village three hours away, where he had gone to get his parents' blessings before the 10-day trip to Java. I needed a massage and she insisted that he would perform it. I am treated to a wonderfully relaxing two-hour deep tissue massage. The owners of the lovely spa, now my friends, insist on not letting me pay for it.

"You are our friend and we are our own bosses. We don't charge you. Please sit."

It's 10:00 p.m., way past the 9:00 p.m. closing time, but they insist that I have a plate of beautifully cut papaya and a cup of hot tea. I feel at peace, my body still floating from the relaxing massage.

I eat at the restaurant next door. Not the atmosphere I'd have chosen, but it's late and I just want to end the day at my own bungalow. The restaurant is big and empty, except for a foreign man in his 60s with a younger Asian woman. He speaks in English, trying to explain to her the financial world crisis. He talks about the 1980s and 1990s, with the specifics. The woman doesn't say a word. She probably doesn't make sense of any of what he is so eager to talk about. It's important to him; it's meaningless to her, it appears. I order, I eat, and I leave. I pass by the rice fields flooded with water. The frogs are loud. They speak different languages, each with an expressive and unique sound. I'm usually afraid of frogs, don't ask me why, but not when I walk by the amphibian-infested rice patties on my way to my bungalow, which is starting to feel like home.

In bed, I think of the Balinese couple from the spa, their hopes, their dreams, their fears, and them saying, "We choose not to charge you. You are our friend."

January 11, 2014 – Another Balinese Day of Yoga, Connections, and Healing

Again I wake up at 2:00 a.m. but I fall back asleep, to wake up again at 6:00 a.m. with a tension headache. I practice the breathing and relaxation I learned during Yoga Nidra. I lie still, breathing in through only one nostril and out the other one. Then I divert my attention to a single part of my body, feeling the energy flow to that area alone. I start with each individual finger of one hand moving slowly to each part and organ of my body. I have practiced this a couple of times very successfully, but this morning I am only partially successful. Maybe I shared way too much last night with the couple, reviving the diagnosis, and the highlights of what has happened in my life for the past year and a half. Maybe I am still hurt by the message I received. Maybe it is all.

I can speak about my diagnosis with ease, but there is probably underlying heaviness deep within, right? If not, I wouldn't wake up with a migraine. But, as I write, I can see sunlight peeking through the sides of the curtains and I become determined to get up and start another day, making it a great one.

After breakfast I go to a Vinyasa Flow class. The class is fast paced, tough, yet the instructor brings breathing and spirituality into it in a holistic and harmonious way.

Tonight there is a special program with nine different musicians, from the Middle East, Chile, Finland, and Hawaii. There is also a Balinese priest in training, and an American dancer. It is an interesting artistic mix and I fully enjoy the night.

The day finishes as most do here in Bali. I hear the frogs in the rice field, and the geckos' squeaks announce that they are somewhere above my head. I light up an incense stick, put mosquito net down, hug my little purple stuffed dragon (that represents LMS), and close my eyes, appreciative of another day.

January 12, 2014 – A Spiritual Day: Travelling to Temple with Tony

Tony invited me to travel to the Mother Temple. The large compound is beautiful and its vibe serene. Because my friend is recognized in Bali as a spiritual "guru", the priest gives as a blessing ceremony as we make offerings of flowers and incense.

On the drive back to Ubud we talk and I share some of the happenings of the past year. He turns to me and says: "You know you are like me, you have a gift. The question is: Do you want to develop it? It requires time and commitment." Well! Again, here is this story about me having a "gift", a deeper intuition. I brush it off, as I have done before.

It was a very special day, one that a tourist usually doesn't get to experience. Again, I feel blessed.

As I crawl into my four-poster bed covered by the mosquito net, I look at the high and pointy woven straw ceiling supported by bamboo. It's a gorgeous ceiling! I feel gratitude for being here, learning to just be. And I close my eyes, ending another blissful day.

"Respond to every call that excites your spirit." — Rumi

FOCUSING ON HELPING CHILDREN HEAL

The reason why I came to Bali in 2012 was to help a child in need of health care. One of the reasons I am now returning is to continue my mission, which has extended to help many children. Through HCH, my small NGO, I started a partnership with the well-established NGO Bali Kids, to provide health care to the children I found with a severe, rare, and life threatening skin disease. There are currently eight children being treated for ichythiosis, including a 7-month-old baby I am meeting today for the first time. We bond instantly.

I feel great relief in knowing that these unfortunate Balinese kids are getting the medical care they need and deserve.

Today I also meet the 9-year-old boy with neurological damage I started sponsoring in 2012, before my own diagnosis of cancer. It broke my heart to find out that 4 years ago he was a normal and happy child, when he had his first seizure; that up to 2 years ago he could walk, and a year ago he could verbally communicate. His mother says the only diagnosis doctors gave him was "seizure" and he never received any form of treatment for anything during the last 4 years. No scans, no physiotherapy or proper nutrition. He never had a wheelchair until I started to sponsor him. He looks malnourished. I understand that there is a possibility that this condition was part of the fate he was determined to have, but deep in my heart I believe this child could have been helped with proper health care. And again, this brings me sadness for his condition, and also gratitude for all the care I have received this year during my own medical journey.

On the way back to Ubud, I reflect on the fact that the day for my departure nears, and I feel that I am not ready to go home yet. The peace and easiness I will leave with are to be confronted with another scan, just days after my return, the routine of work, and facing pending issues. But reality calls and I must go.

January 18, 2014 – Last Day in Bali

I had lunch with people I can call real friends, those I already had a connection to since 2012, and a couple I met during this trip. It was a joyful time, but there was a hidden feeling of longing, since we will be in different continents until God knows when.

I spent time with Nina and on my way to a last massage at Jaen Spa; I stop to contemplate a magnificent sunset. I think of a friend back home how enjoys sunsets just as much as I do.

The moments I lived today, and during all the other days here in Bali will be added to my collection of memorable times worth treasuring. I must now go pack, as tomorrow morning I say goodbye to this enchanting island.

During the drive to the airport, I think of the passages on the The Alchemist, which talks about one's "personal legend", or life calling. "What's my own personal legend?" I wonder. I guess for many years it was to have a happy family and raise the children well. Then, added to that, it was to find and help poor children with unmet medical needs, and to respond to my urge to explore the world, getting to experience other cultures first hand, just like Santiago from The Alchemist. I have the sense that I have yet more callings in this life, and I must believe I will be granted the time and health to make them happen. Only time can review that, right? For now, I hope.

"I believe in everything until it's disproved. So I believe in fairies, the myths, dragons. It all exists, even if it's in your mind. Who's to say that dreams and nightmares aren't as real as the here and now?" — John Lennon

BACK IN THE USA FOR 9-MONTH CHECKUP

My main reason for returning from Bali was my every-three-months commitment to the CT-scanner. I have a sort of love-hate relationship with the machine. I hate that cancer knocked on my life and entered my body, and that I have to be radiated after getting toxic dye; but although I don't love it, I am grateful that there is such a machine that can detect if the bastard comes back.

After my time in Indonesia, I've felt confident, until the day before the exam. I heard from my Californian friend who was diagnosed with lung carcinoma five months ago. She went through chemotherapy and radiation and her prognosis was supposed to be good. Now the darn cancer shows up in her brain and spinal cord. I felt incredible sadness for her, and fear took hold of me again. It's hard not to think that this is a sneaky and deadly disease that can rob you of your life, in no time.

As the tears start to roll down, I decide to practice what I preach to others:

"Exercise can help with stress and anxiety, particularly when you have no drive to do it." So, I head to a belly dancing class, and feel a better afterwards.

January 22, 2014 – Test Day

The morning comes and I drink the barium at 7:00 a.m. I have decided that I'm going to get the scan alone, as I have learned that if the company you have is not supportive, it is better to face it on your own. However, as I drive out on a freezing morning, I find myself under the most beautiful blue sky, the sun to my back and the moon just ahead. "I am not alone; I am with the Universe," I think, with a smile. And I drive forward, physically alone, but spiritually connected to it all.

I was calm during the test and I walked out with serenity within. Listening to Deva Premal, I headed to Cymplify Cafe. I find myself in the "now." Tomorrow will come with test results, but at this present moment, it is just I and the warmth of my cup of coffee. Today, I cultivate the now and my passion for life.

Sadness and comtemplation by the lake, dissapointed at my intuition and the Universe.

"The unexpected can take you out. But the unexpected can also take you over and change your life." — Ron Hall

JANUARY 23, 2014 - UNEXPECTED SHIFT: THE DRAGON AWAKENS

My intuition that all is fine, that my body is healthy and cancer free is crushed in a split second. The doctor walks into the small room and asks if I have any symptoms, like cough. I know at that instant something is wrong, and it is: five lesions (tumors) were found in my lungs. THE DRAGON HAS AWAKENED.

I look up at the ceiling, trying to find reasons from the Universe. I feel numb, suspended in an unreal time and space. My mouth murmurs an agonizing and low "No," followed by another. Tears roll down my face. I'm in shock, in complete disbelief. The way my mind, body, and spirit felt, just a fraction of a second ago, doesn't match this reality being told. How can I feel so alive, so filled with energy, vitality, enthusiasm, and yet have a deadly cancer spreading inside me, eating my body away? It doesn't make sense. I am brutally disappointed. I feel helpless.

The doctor says he hopes the spots are false positive since I just returned from Bali. They could be an infection or virus. Thus, he suggests I have a biopsy to confirm. Fear sneaks in again, but I want this done a.s.a.p.

My friend Martha waits outside. I step out and as I hug her, I cry and cry. I call my sister Andrea in Brazil, the words coming out as desperately as the sobbing and the rolling tears. She says she will fly in the next day to be by my side, although she also believes the lesions are false positive.

The next day my oncologist calls telling me that the scheduled biopsy has been cancelled because the specialist found that the bigger nodule wasn't accessible. A PET scan is then ordered.

January 27-28, 2014 - More Surreal News

Andrea, John and I head to the oncology clinic for the PET scan. I am calm, somehow. I even drift away as I meditate, waiting for the injected dye to do its job.

The next day the three of us return for the results, all with diverse magnitudes of hope. The oncologist walks in and it didn't take long for him to announce, "I am so sorry. There's metastasis to the liver also: Five extra nodules."

What a shock!!! Another unexpected blow on my path that feels completely surreal. The reality I feel within doesn't match the medical reality reviewed to me. This doesn't make any sense, God. Why? Why? Why?

I feel the blood leaving my face as I'm told there is a new trial going on at Mayo Clinic, which includes two chemotherapy drugs plus a study drug, an antibody, which two-thirds of patients will get. The other one-third will be randomized to a placebo. I murmur that I will consider it, thinking to myself: *What other choice do I have?*

How can this be happening? I feel so healthy. I have done so much! Even going to Brazil to see John of God. The fierce Dragon is still spreading. *Why, God? Why?*

As the doctor steps out, I turn to my husband, with much anger: "Are you out of denial now? Are you?" I cry hard on my sister's shoulder and even harder deep inside my heart. *Metastasis, chemotherapy, randomized trial. I am devastated, shattered.*

On the silent drive home, I think of my kids. Oh God, how I wish I could give them good news and spare them these painful ones. But the truth can't be hidden, and when I arrive home, with a stream of tears flowing, I give them the awful and serious news, promising them I will fight hard to win the battle, even though at the moment I have no strength. I am just numb inside.

The oncologist at Mayo calls me and discusses the trial and its protocol.

Close friends come to the house. I cry on every shoulder offered to me as I invite sadness deep within my being. I ask Gideon, a scientist, to review the protocol. I am in no shape to read or make any decision. My friend Joy called another oncologist, and also my friend and physician, Ed, who also has cancer. Gideon discussed the protocol with them, and I made the decision to enroll in the trial right then.

I take the Valium the doctor prescribed and I am able to have pizza with family and close friends, but I just want to vanish, disappear. I am screaming silently inside. I wish this day, this news, and this reality were all but a dream, a nightmare I could wake up from. I don't want to think, to feel. I am desolated.

I wake up the next day and all I want is to *fly* to a place that feels like a safe nest. I want to be held tight, to succumb to a dreamy state, to watch the smoke of incense dance with a ray of sunshine. I want to flee from this sickening reality that wants to drop me down, to swallow dreams, my life, my being.

"Bravery is being terrified and doing it anyway." — Laurell K. Hamilton

JANUARY 30, 2014 - ANOTHER NEW BEGINNING: TREATMENT TO TAME/SLAY THE DRAGON

A couple of days later I'm at the Mayo Clinic meeting the study coordinator and oncologist, and signing up for the trial, with the support of the loved ones who packed the doctor's room beyond capacity: Gideon, Joy, Andrea, Amanda, John, and myself.

I let Gideon do the questioning about the trial. I am quite passive, thinking that at this point, I don't have options. I've surrendered. But I ask the doctor a couple of questions:

"How long will the treatments last?"

"Nine months, a year, a year and a half, or until you give up," he answers.

That last part of the sentence cuts right through my heart. At that moment, it sounded like "It will be so hard, you might not stand it, and give it up." Later, however, I am able to think: *"I'll tolerate it and it will work, you will see."*

"Can I still go on my already booked trip to Brazil in four months (to see John of God and then for vacation with my family during the World Cup)?"

The "No." came instantaneously.

"Could I go just for five days?" I bargained.

Another "No." is heard.

That one little word saddened me. Later, I burst out crying, realizing that cancer was taking more things from me. Now it goes my ability to travel.

Back at the hotel, I started to look at wigs on the Internet, as I had been told that hair loss is an expected side effect of the chemo drugs I will get. Fun at first, with my sister and Amanda giving their opinions, but all of a sudden it felt too real. The reality of The Dragon and chemotherapy set in hard.

"I don't want to be choosing wigs," I said desolately. "I don't want the diagnosis of cancer, I don't want any of this." I burst into tears as I proceed to lock myself in the bathroom. I sit on the floor and I sob for along time. I am so sad. I feel so lost and alone.

February 1-9, 2014 - What a Roller Coaster Ride!

The next day I am in the operating room, having a port implanted below my right collarbone. I handle the procedure well and somehow I am in good spirits going in and coming out of the hospital. I get a lovely message from a person dear to my heart, and it makes me dream of going back to Bali. A ray of light reaches my heart.

Three days later I have an MRI. So many tests within one week, but I would have many more if they just didn't show lesions lighting up! This latest test is the longest and noisiest of them all. Despite having had all the recent bad news, somehow I don't need any help from Valium.

The roller coaster of emotional ups and downs starts all over again, like when I was diagnosed nine months ago. One minute I feel peaceful, accepting and hopeful, the next I burst out crying uncontrollably, feeling that the freaking Dragon is taking control of my life. MY LIFE!

Doubts, so many doubts are ahead. Will the chemo work? How will the side effects be? Will I get the antibody? How long will the treatments last? What's going to happen to my health, my lifestyle, my life, and my dreams? So much uncertainty!

By now I know I don't have the luxury to be down and negative, and I understand positivity has to be exercised full force. Thus, I get determined. *"I will get the antibody and it will work, it will work, it will work..."* becomes my mantra. I must believe.

The peace of Bali seems to have happened ages ago, yet it has only been a few days since I returned from paradise. And so it is. And so it is.

"Gratitude is not only the greatest of virtues,
but the parent of all others." — Cicero

UNEXPECTED OUTPOURING OF PRAYERS AND SUPPORT: HOW CAN I BE SO BLESSED?

On the days that followed, and up to now, an outpouring of messages of support and prayers has flooded my soul. Most are posted on Facebook. Brazilian family and friends I have not seen in decades, as far back as middle-school, have joined a healing group of prayers to happen each day and time I have chemo.

Two Brazilian friends I last met more than 30 years ago started the loving and caring movement. American, Indian, Balinese, Australian, British friends, and more, have joined in. I have been overtaken by love, feeling so humbled and grateful. Now, for the first time, I have to acknowledge that The Dragon is indirectly showering me with the gift of love. Wow! Did I just write that? Yes, I did, and this is unexpectedly amazing.

People write about my strength, about me making them strong, calling me a warrior! It sounds so odd, as I still don't consider myself particularly courageous, and I draw courage from them. But it's not worth to dwell on who does what, and I accept that a symbiotic relationship has been created; the energy of strength flows both ways, and we all thrive on it.

Whenever possible, my spirit *flies to a tree house* to find comfort, peace, and love. I dare to dream, as it keeps me awake and alive. I get the charge to feel hopeful that a healthier tomorrow is around the corner. I must believe, and so I do.

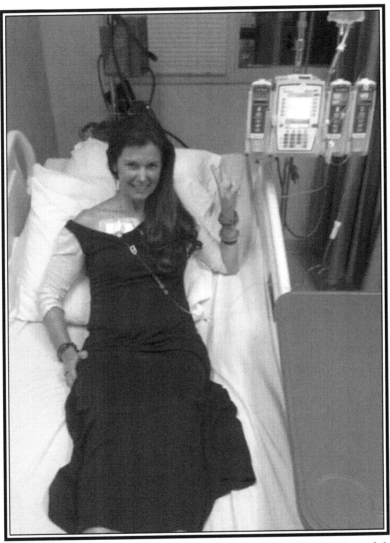

Receiving first chemo practicing positivity, feeling well, and hopeful that it will work.

"Courage is grace under pressure." — Ernest Hemingway

CHEMO: DIVE INTO THE UNKNOWN

All medical tests show that I have this deadly disease inside me, even though I don't feel a single symptom. I feel physically healthy. The pain has only been felt in my own heart and the hearts of those who love me. Here I am, diving into the unknown, about to have chemotherapy. It will affect my body negatively, but hopefully positively as well, as it is *the one* weapon I have against The Dragon. The focus is on hope.

I was apprehensive about receiving chemo in the first place, as I didn't know how my body might handle it. I want as many of my supporting team as possible there. I do not want to feel alone. Yes, I am a little scared. I am scared! So, the night before the first treatment, we are five heading to Jacksonville: Robina, Joy, John, and my sister, Andrea.

Surprisingly, when the morning came, I felt somehow ready. As I settle on the bed on the chemotherapy wing at Mayo, I realize I will receive treatment for seven hours, while monitored closely with regular EKGs and temperature checks. I spread my good luck charms (A Balinese Ganesh that Tony gave me, a crystal from Abadiânia, and a bracelet from a friend), besides dark chocolate-covered cranberries, my mascot Dragon, the little magic bell that *transports* me to the trails I love, and a *Life* magazine of amazing places to visit before one dies. The hours pass by faster than expected and I react so well during treatment that we drive back to Gainesville. I lie on the back seat for the two-hour drive and get home very tired.

The following day was supposed to be the worst as far as gastrointestinal reaction goes, but I wake up feeling really well.

Hooray! And so it goes during the days leading to the party I have been planning. Yes, a big purple benefit party at my home, five days after chemo started! The oncologist was hesitant about it at first, but gave me the okay, as long as it happens this week.

"Life has its own hidden forces which you can only discover by living." — Soren Kierkegaard

MY BIRTHDAY AND MY BIGGEST GIFTS: LOVED ONES AND FUNDRAISER FOR LMS RESEARCH

My friends Robina, Joy, Martha and Michelle, together with my family, help me to put together a "Purple Dragon Benefit" to raise funds for LMS research. We planned it last minute, just before chemo started. It is to be held on February 15, my birthday, and I want nothing else as a gift.

My mother, brother-in-law, and cousin Monica flew in from Brazil. Three dear friends came from California, and three from South Florida. I am surrounded by love. The tears come and go. I have been on chemo for five days, and here I am, with over 100 people dressed in purple, supporting the cause I have embraced.

It was really wonderful to see the number of people who traveled from near and far to attend and show their support. I felt so humbled and thankful. "If you had any doubts about your supporters before your party, I think you can feel confident now that you have an army of supporters," Robina tells me. And so I felt.

The event was a success, with plenty of food, drinks, prizes, donations and, above all, love. I let it permeate my heart and every cell in my body. I feel happiness, bliss.

It was 11:00 p.m. when most guests had left the party and I headed to the restroom. I look down and see that my thighs are covered with a red rash. I rush out, filled with hope, but uncertain.

I meet my sister on the hallway and blast: "I have bad, but I guess it might be actually good news. What did the doctor say about rash?" "That the people getting the rash might be the ones getting

146

the study drug." I asked the others who were at the appointment as well. Everyone agreed that some people on the trial have developed skin rashes, and those could be the ones getting the antibody. So, I end my birthday receiving yet another gift and proclaiming out loud, "I LOVE RASHES!"

After all guests leave, the euphoria of the event winds down and I am tired. I've been on the go, non-stop, since the day I got the news about the metastasis, or should I say, since I left Bali 28 days ago? I say *"boa noite"* (good night) and with joy in my heart, I go to sleep.

Today, I celebrated life.

February 18, 2014: Second Chemo Session

I wake up to messages of *"bom dia"* (good morning) and of prayers and positive thought being sent my way. I don't feel alone, and this means the world to me.

For this second chemo session, we again pack the room, now including my cousin Monica. The doctor seems content with the news and sight of my rash. He couldn't say, of course, but it appears I am getting the antibody. Feeling confident and cheerful, I tell him, "Write it down. I'll need only a few rounds of treatment, and we will make history." He just smiles.

Having loved ones by my side on the trips and duration of the chemo sessions has been vital. I don't feel alone, I get distracted, and the time passes quicker. I have so much gratitude for having family and friends with me, as the love received is priceless and makes it all more manageable, doable.

Whenever fear tries to poke in, I hold one of my amulets tightly, and let my mind fly far away, where it can find comfort and hope. I pray.

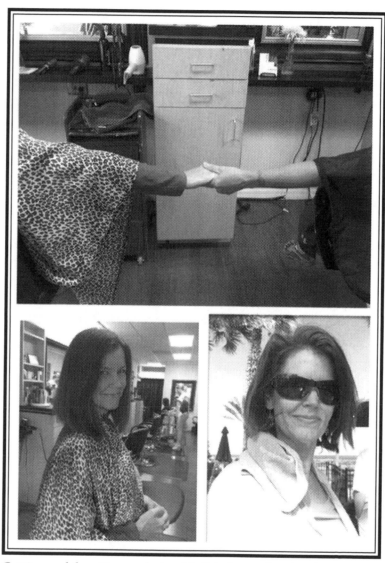

Cutting and donating my hair with Cristiane, who also donated hers in solidarity to me.

"In love, all fear dissolves. There is no fear." — Brian Weiss, M.D

WIG SHOPPING & DONATING MY HAIR

When I told the doctor I was going to donate my hair to Locks of Love, he said, "In this case you'd better cut it this week because by next week it will be too late."

Although I knew my hair would fall, I didn't expect it to be this fast. Determined to donate it, I make the appointment for the cut for my friend Cristiane and I. She decided to donate her hair in solidarity to me. What a beautiful gesture of love!

The day before the cut I go shopping for wigs with Andrea and Joy, and surprisingly, I don't handle it too well. I can't pinpoint the exact feeling, but there is uneasiness within. With a wig on, the image I see reflected in the mirror is the reality of The Dragon and not ME. This image I see doesn't match how I feel inside. I have a hard time looking in the mirror. I leave the store without any wigs, and suddenly, I have a massive migraine.

The day before I had an injection of leunasta, a medicine to stimulate the bone marrow to produce fighting white blood cells. I was told about the probable side effects expected within 24 to 48 hours. So, I go to bed thinking the migraine was all about the wigs, but soon I am shivering under the covers and have a fever of 101.7, despite taking Aleve. The doctor calls in a prescription for antibiotics.

I was in bed with fever for 13 hours, but by the next mid-morning I sat in the chair at the salon, my friend Lauren with scissors in hand. Cristiane and I hold hands as we have our long locks cut. It was an amazing feeling of letting go. Although I had never had short hair in my life, this cut had the purpose to help a child with cancer get a wig, and that made me happy. I embraced the new look fully, and so did Cris. Worth it! One point for you darn Dragon.

"Your task is not to seek for love, but merely to seek and find all the barriers within yourself you have built against it." — Rumi

LEARNING TO RECEIVE AND SHINE

Shortly after my diagnosis, when I started to listen to Louise Hay and others on the subject of healing, learning to receive was always on the list of top things to be done. So, I started to practice receiving, along with slowing down, taking time off without guilt, making yoga and meditation a priority, et cetera.

Learning to receive has been, without a doubt, the greatest, and also one of the hardest lessons the diagnosis of cancer has taught me. I never realized that I must not have had much practice at it, as it was so difficult to receive at first, and up to today I still feel some uneasiness.

Surrendering to the much-needed shoulders to cry on wasn't very hard. I needed them desperately, and feeling bad to be burdening people faded away. Accepting help with household responsibilities wasn't that difficult. Receiving the outpouring of prayers sent my way was humbling, and in time I learned to embrace it and just thank each person.

However, I still don't know what to do with the compliments coming my way. I feel embarrassed, awkward. Although I am aware that I am a nice person, I don't feel I have done nearly enough to deserve as much praise as I have received. Also, although I have come a very long way from the childhood days when I was made to believe I was fairly ugly (ha-ha!), to receive the compliments I have received also about my physical appearance still makes me uncomfortable.

While talking about the subject of receiving with Jennifer, who is the most serene and spiritual friend I have ever had, and who has taught me so much during this journey, she tells me: "Think of receiving a compliment as a practice of receiving. The compliment is a gift. Imagine the person who is complimenting you as the bearer of this gift, holding it out to you. By receiving this gift, you allow the energy of kindness to be exchanged. What you do with the gift is up to you; whether you hold onto it, savor it, embody it, or let it go, is up to you. But without you as receiver in that moment, the kindness, the thoughtfulness, and the love do not complete; the energy does not move."

Jennifer later sends me an email, which says, "This is one of my favorite poems. It aligns with what you are journaling about this week." And it does. So, I'm sharing part of it here.

Our Deepest Fear
    "We ask ourselves,
    Who am I to be brilliant, gorgeous, handsome, talented
and fabulous?
    Actually, who are you not to be?"

    "And, as we let our own light shine, we consciously give
other people permission to do the same."
                        - Marianne Williamson, A Return to Love

February 26, 2014: Enjoying the Week Off-Chemo

On the drive to Mayo, Andrea and I laughed all the way. I put on a Brazilian music CD from long ago, and that opened up the door of our memories to fun times of all sorts. Our childhood and teenage years came back to life.

It all went smoothly at my appointment and my results were good. Alleluia! How grateful I am that my body is reacting well so far, and, hopefully, for the long haul. I share the good news with family and Facebook followers. They have come to be such an integral part of my "team."

We then drove to Palm Coast to stay at a friend's beach condo for the week. We arrived in the evening, tired but content. We crashed, after another long day. I meditated and prayed that I would finally have a full night of sleep.

Well, that didn't quite happen. Three hours into the night, I am awake. I put on a guided sleep meditation in the hopes that I wouldn't need a second sleeping pill, but it was to no avail. An hour later I am taking another pill, just to wake up again after two hours. I don't get upset with my body anymore if I can't get the much-needed restorative sleep I need to heal. I try my very best to sleep, by creating the best environment and conditions, but if I still wake up, I just accept and hope that the next night will be better.

The beach is magically peaceful. There is quietness for meditation and just being present with nature all around. It's a change of scenery that does me good.

The chemo side effects are subsiding and I am able to go to the gym, take yoga classes, and enjoy the taste of food again, no longer metallic. It all feels amazing.

During the weekend, my kids come to visit. Amanda and I have a harsh encounter, which in the end was for the better, as it allowed us to express our bottled up feelings about how we are emotionally handling my diagnosis. I had been somewhat concerned that she was still in denial. She shared that she has been venting with her friends, that she cries all her tears, that she knows the seriousness of the situation, but makes the effort not to bring negative energy to me. In moments like this I hate cancer; I hate The Dragon. We both cried, and although we didn't totally lighten up that night, by the next day we were joyfully enjoying the homemade and delicious waffles she made for Andrea and me. I am in the company of the two women I love the most in the whole world, and that is a great reason to celebrate life.

"*Happiness is not something ready made. It comes from your own actions.*" Dalai Lama.

"No one ever loses anyone. We are all one soul that needs to continue growing and developing in order for the world to carry on and for us all to meet once again." — Paulo Coelho, *Aleph*

... AND CANCER TAKES FRIENDS AWAY

Within one week I lost two friends to cancer. They were both diagnosed after me and battled the darn disease bravely.

Chester has been an amazing and close friend for 10 years. Older than me, he and I had one of those special brotherly connections. We got each other, we had admiration for each other, and somehow we always knew when one needed to reach the other. So many times I'd ring him just to hear the best laughter I have ever heard on the other side, followed by "My hand was on the phone to call you. How did you know?"

The same would happen when I was thinking of him: the phone would ring, and I would already know what to expect. I would say, "Oh my God, I was thinking about calling you just now!" I'd then have the pleasure of hearing his laugher over again.

When I was at MD Anderson Cancer Center in Houston, he texted me: "When you get back, it's my time to fly to Houston." I thought he was going to visit his sister, also named Patricia. But we met for coffee at Starbucks, as we had so many times before, and he shared that a mass had been discovered on his pancreas. Our friend Pat and I took him to the airport in late July 2013. Right before I started chemo I got a message that he had been given a week or two to live. I called him from the car on my way to Mayo for my first chemo. It was an amazing conversation that lasted almost an hour. We wondered about how in the hell both of us ended up with cancer at the same time, we talked about not giving up, and about making the pack to be *"in touch"*, *NO MATTER WHERE WE ARE*. We both knew we were referring to when we were in two *different planes*, as we were aware that time was running out for him here on Earth. He said that he always wished that he would be given plenty of time (before dying), and he was glad he was given that. He also shared that he was happy he had reconciled with his brother and that the two got really close during his time of need. The most amazing thing is that I found myself saying over and over again, "That's my Chester!" at the sound of each one of his famous laughs. My heart found comfort in the memories of that warm and heartfelt last conversation, when five days later he passed away. I know he left in peace. I feel I have to keep on fighting harder than ever.

Just five days after Chester passed away, I got the news that Melisa, my college friend, had also passed away. She was diagnosed with small cell lung carcinoma just six months ago and we had been in touch, rooting for each other. I wrote to her family and said I'll keep fighting for myself and in her honor, as well as in Chester's honor.

My eyes are dry, my heart tight, and my whole being is determined not to give in to the brutal Dragon, and to draw the forces of the Universe to win for myself and to give hope to others. On the battlefield with the beast, one can prevail as a winner; and I will.

"The secret of being happy is accepting where you are in life and making the most out of everyday." — Unknown

TOLERATING TREATMENT & ENJOYING LIFE

The day before my second round of treatment is perfect! I feel no side effects of the treatment; I feel amazing, happy, and light. The Oscar review is the buzz and Brazilian Carnival is going on full force, but all the costumes, riches, dancing, glitter, and partying, don't match being in my PJs, reading, writing, eating, and chatting with my sister.

Late morning we ventured out to enjoy the magnificence of the day: the sky was a calming blue; the sun shone warm; the birds chirped, and the ocean breeze was just cool enough. We go for a walk on the beach, chatting, laughing, and holding hands, just goofing around. The seagulls and pelicans are teased by the gentle waves, completing the landscape. We play with our shadows, take pictures, and I do yoga while overlooking the ocean which seemed to stretch to the infinite, as it merged with the horizon somewhere far, far away.

This day was glorious for Andrea and me, and I couldn't be more thankful for that. I share the memories of the day with a friend and say *boa noite*, as I turn the light off and go to sleep. Today, I chose to embrace enthusiasm and repel sadness and fear.

March 4, 2014 - Second Round of Chemo Starts and I Am Still Holding On

I spent six marvelous days at the beach. I felt full of vitality, going for walks and yoga at the beach, and to the gym. I felt healthy, well, and The Dragon appeared to be just a phantom. Feeling 100% well,

156

it seemed surreal that we were driving to Mayo again, for the third chemo session. How can I feel this good and be going to get chemo, which will poison my body? It doesn't seem real, it just doesn't.

The oncologist reports that my blood cell counts are still good, but should change in seven days. (We will see, right? Just maybe, they won't.)

I record a short video and post it on Facebook, to show my friends and family that I am well, and to thank them again for their unbelievable support and prayers. Shortly after, I felt a funny sensation in my body. The nurse adjusted down the infusion rate of the study drug. I felt sleepy and rested. When the session was done we met with John and Amanda for dinner and drove the two hours back home. I was very tired, at the end of another long day. But the most important thing is that I am still at peace and hopeful. Amen to that.

March 5, 2014 – Spiritual Surgery at Home

My brother traveled to the Casa in Abadiânia to request a spiritual surgery for me. I didn't expect it was going to be on that day, and was surprised when I read his message that it had just happened. I knew that I had to rest for 24 hours, as if in a recovery room, and stay away from electronics. And so I did. I prayed. I meditated. I opened myself up to receive divine blessing. I chose to believe!

*"You have to fight through some bad days to earn
the best days of your life." — Unknown*

A Gloomy Day and Losing My Hair

Today is a very gloomy day. It rained hard all morning, and I have no desire to think or to move. I just want to lay in bed, inert. I don't know if it's just the weather or if it is something deeper within. It is just incredibly unusual that I don't want to get up.

By mid-afternoon, the bedroom is still dark, just like I feel inside. I can hear my sister outside my room. "Is she on a hunger strike?"

I eventually get up to shower and my hair just washes off my head. I knew it would happen, but why on this gloomy day? Why couldn't it be when I don't feel so gray, and all spark has left my soul?

I drag myself around all day, without an appetite or desire to do anything, including talking or smiling. Later, my sister and I wonder if maybe, just maybe, the spiritual surgery had something to do with it. The fascinating mysteries of the unknown...

While in bed in the morning, I played *The Cancion del Silencio* (the song of silence) a dozen times. Now, at the end of the day, I still desire to listen to the silence screaming inside of me to be heard. I miss the companionship of my traveller within.

I go to bed and read *'Proof of Heaven'* until I am really sleepy. I wake up four hours later and play guided meditation until my conscious mind finally fades away.

March 7, 2014 - There is Always Another Day, Potentially Brighter

I wake up early and find myself wanting to write. A couple of hours later I am ready to get up, wearing a smile, greeting the new day and my sister. My happy and hopeful self is back. I want to dream of travelling far, far away.

March 8, 2014 - What a Mix of Emotions! What a Bumpy Journey!

The sun came out and the sky is a divine blue. I announce to my sister that we must go out and make the most of the gorgeous day.

We head to a charming area in town where there is an organic farmer's market on Saturdays. First, we sit at a café, enjoying a warm latte by the small plaza where preparations are going on for an outdoor wedding ceremony. Dogs passing by fascinate Ziggy. A friend drops by for coffee and a chat. What a stunning day to be lived! I repeat this several times and my whole being rejoices with gratitude.

But later, an encounter manages to get me off balance. An argument about finances hits me hard. I don't feel ready to focus on accounting for tax filing. That sounds so unimportant, dry, lifeless, and I just don't want to spend precious moments with that, although I understand the importance of it, as taxes will go on being declared and collected, despite cancer/The Dragon.

Discussing finances strikes me hard as the new reality that I no longer generate an income hits me square in the face. I have worked since I was 20, becoming a successful dietitian, and now, the doors of my office are shut. I'm not financially independent for the first time in my adult life, and cancer is to blame; another thing the freaking Dragon has taken away from me.

One more incident by the end of the day adds the last drop to my full bucket, and by 11:00 p.m., it overflows with tears. I vent to my sister. "How can an amazing day be ending filled with a hurtful sense of loss? Ah The Dragon!" I cry for not working. I cry because I don't like how I was treated. I cry because I know that I have been avoiding combing my hair because if I just pass my fingers through my head, a handful of hair will simply detach.

With tears wetting my cheeks, I comb and witnessed the inevitable: ALL my hair is falling out. I won't have the cute pixie cut in two days, as planned.

Tonight I honor the needs of my soul... and I'm still crying as I get a wig out of a bag. How I wish the day was ending as it started, but perfection doesn't always happen... and I go brush my teeth.

March 9, 2014 – Glorious Sunday

The day exudes pure bliss. It's sunny, warm, and beautiful. After walking with Ziggy to a friend's house for a coffee, the day presented me with a couple of surprises.

The drive to a nearby small town through the back roads, lined up with old oak trees covered with Spanish moss, was peaceful, enjoyable. After a tasty lunch outdoors, walking by a store, I hear: "Patricia. Do you want to check this out?" I turned around and see a sign on a small table on the sidewalk. "Ring for prayer." My friend rings and soon we find ourselves in front of an African-American man who says: "What can I do for you? Who needs prayer?"

After glancing at me to see if it would be all right, my friend answers: "Patricia has cancer."

The man turns to me and asks if I believe in God. I nod and he says to follow him. He gets a bottle of an orange liquid, pours some of it on his hand and then on my forehead. He then holds our hands, making a circle, and prays out loud asking for me to be healed.

I feel connected and grateful for the unexpected happening. Tears wet my eyes, but not of sadness. I feel blessed, touched by the encounter, the moment of connection and hope. Thank you my dear friend for sharing this day with me! You don't know how much you have given me, do you?

a) Day I shaved my head. b) Embrace by my sister Andrea. c) Wearing purple wig with my daughter Amanda, who shaved part of her hair. d) Being kissed by my son Yannick.

"Bravery is being terrified and doing it anyway." — Laurell K. Hamilton

SHAVING MY HEAD

Today marks one month since treatment started and The Dragon teaches me about total acceptance of who I truly am: essence and spirit. I want life, to live, but I surrender completely to Divine order and wishes. Today I am, for the first time, not afraid of death.

This morning, my friend and hairdresser Lauren will come by to shave the 20% of hair still attached to my scalp. Any trace of vanity is gone, as I look like a character from *Lord of the Rings*, mostly bald with a few odd patches of hair.

I easily surrender to the shaving blade, without attachment to my hair. With my head already shaved, I look in the mirror, and I feel I am simply who I am. I am spirit, essence, and consciousness. I am what lies within, and hair is just hair.

March 11, 2014 - Chemo Without Hair But in High Spirits

Up at 5:30 a.m. for the two-hour drive to Mayo Clinic with my sister and Joy. I lie in the back seat since I only got a few hours of sleep. The uneasiness snuck in last night. But now the cellphone blings announcing I have a new message: "You are in my thoughts and prayers today." My heart and soul rejoices. I'll be okay.

I arrive feeling fresh and in good spirits, wearing a goofy blue hat, with Furby's face and ears on it. People comment on it and smile. It feels good to spread smiles in a setting which, although physically beautiful, exudes the sorrow of illness.

My blood counts start to get off normal ranges but are still considered very good for a body assaulted by the poison that is chemo. At the group prayer time, when friends from around the globe will be sending positive healing vibes my way, I lie receiving the drugs, meditating on my full healing. I think positively to myself. *I won't need but a few rounds of chemotherapy. This treatment, together with the powerful force within me, and also the vibes of the Universe, will cure this dis-ease in me. The Dragon came out of nowhere and should return to nowhere.*

The trial coordinator comes in several times to check my vitals and do EKGs. I chat happily and she turns to my sister, asking: "Is she always so energetic?"

My sister answers, "Yes. Usually even more than this."

As we are again alone, my sister says, "See. That's why I say that you are the one who makes us strong, not the other way around."

I feel ready to post pictures of me without hair on Facebook. The outpouring of support was nothing short of extraordinary. So many heartfelt messages humble me. I feel naked, as if I have shed every layer between the contour of my physical body and my core. I am my soul, I am spirit, and I feel blessed.

"Coincidence is God's way of remaining anonymous." — Albert Einstein

ANOTHER COINCIDENCE?

A woman writes to me: "Can we talk? I really would like to." I don't recognize her name, and opening her profile on Facebook, I see that she is from Portugal. I don't know anyone in Portugal, so I get curious and accept her as a FB friend. She thanks me for my posts, saying she is praying for me, and sharing that her son had LMS. I answer, saying that I am sorry, and asking how he is doing. How sad it was to read her reply that he had passed away at age 19 of testicular LMS, being only one in seven people ever reported with this type of cancer in the world. Wow! The Dragon is fierce, sneaky, selective, and exquisite!

During the next days she continues to write, clearly still in the process of grieving, after seven years of loss, and looking for support, help. I share with her that "I lost my first son, and that I learned to let him go only this past year in Abadiânia. I was chosen to be his mother just during pregnancy, as she was chosen to be her son's mother for 19 years."

After writing long messages, she writes a short question: "Are you from Maceió, Brazil?" I answer yes, but I have been in the USA for many years. Now she writes again, "I saw you are a friend of Ana Sofia, from Maceió. She is my cousin!" Wow. What a coincidence! Just another among many, right? And I smile, remembering Dr. Weiss telling me, "There are no coincidences. You synchronize and channel." And so it is.

"Life is like a roller coaster. It has its ups and downs. But it's your choice to scream or enjoy the ride." — Unknown

SEESAW OF EMOTIONS

The day drags from uneasiness within. I know the reason, and it is related to The Dragon, but I'm reminded several times that chemo can affect your mood as well, and to be gentle with myself.

I decide to go to the gym, for the first time since the metastasis appeared. The always-cheerful Ricky, the spinning instructor, passes by without recognizing me. I have no hair and a cap on. I get his attention; he comes to give me a hug, and asks how things are going. Tears wet both of our eyes. I take a few steps and Joseph, my Zumba teacher, sees me and runs to give me a big hug. Now the tears are rolling down freely. His hair has grown since he shaved it when his sister's cancer hit hard. I said that now it was my turn, and he says, "This will be it and you will beat this, you will see."

I move on to the machines and quickly can feel my heart pounding very hard. Soon, my muscles feel shaky. Where is my strength? Not in my body today, so I leave, and sit in the car for a while, letting time pass, letting myself just be.

In the evening, friends who have been supportive during this journey came by for pizza, salad, and wine. I wanted to thank them, and show how appreciative I am of each one of them. It's the first time they see me hairless but all goes well. They bring up the subject of medical marijuana, as a talked-about viable alternative to cancer treatment. I say I don't have side effects, thank God, but if they do research and find it can help with the tumors, I will consider it.

March 15, 2014 - Friendship: Does The Dragon Give Just to Take Away?

The drive through the back roads is so enjoyable. The moss dropping from gigantic oak trees displays nature's partnership. Arriving at a small sleepy town, I enjoy a meal outdoors. What I order looks good but it tastes bland, like nothing, courtesy of chemo side effects. But, with a little mustard, ketchup and lemon, I eat each one of the calories needed by my body, since I have lost weight. I am grateful that food doesn't taste metallic or bitter, like three weeks before. However, I am silently sad within. I feel loneliness even when in company. I wish it was different; I wish things wouldn't change; I wish The Dragon would vanish forever, and let me be free, to enjoy a joyful partnership...

I hate the Dragon at this moment, as it seems to have the power to transform fulfilling relationships, possibly making people feel like a parasite has manifested to disrupt the carefree nature of times shared. Maybe, the Dragon is overwhelmingly scary to my buddy, appearing contagious, with the power to rob his liveliness as well.

On the drive back, there is silence, but I then hear the oak trees whispering to me. "At times, the Spanish moss feels as a parasite clinging to me. I fear I may be overtaken by it; the freedom of my branches may be robbed and light may be obscured."

I do not want to feel like a parasite. I want the partnership felt one day, the beauty of a symbiotic relationship. "Dragon, are you taking it away? Please don't. Please. don't."

"A ship is safe in harbor, but that's not what ships are for." — William G.T. Shedd

PRACTICING COURAGE BY ZIP LINING

It is a glorious morning. I contemplate the beauty outside and enjoy my sister's and Ziggy's company. Each new day is a blessing and I fully intend to make this one unforgettable.

Micanopy is a charming old town where I have enjoyed some of the most blissful moments during the past months. It's quiet, mysterious, and has a certain magic porch, where time remains still, and the outside world and cancer become non-existent. The old sofa is magical; it grounds me in the now, while I am enjoying a latte and the candid spirit by me. Time flies at the porch, but how, today, I wish it would just stand still.

I meet a friend who has invited me to go zip lining in a town nearby. Where is my fear? It's nowhere to be found. And so I head to Ocala, determined to practice some courage. The views are gorgeous, the height from the cables to the quarry, very high. But hey! If I'm strong enough to fight The Dragon, I can't fear this, right?

I soon realize that the zip-line harness includes a strap dropping from both shoulders, right where my port is. Ha, another reminder of the chemo and a possible limitation. Darn it!

I approach one of the guides and explain my situation. He finds the owner, who brings some gauze for padding and tape. He shares that he's a cancer survivor and announces that I'm going to be all right.

The freedom to hang fearlessly, letting go of it all, is empowering, energizing. True surrender. As I hang, feet above the ground, going at 25 miles per hour, beauty all around, and crystal water below, I speak to the Universe: "Please give me my health and a cure." Soon, the request turns into a proclamation. *I am healthy and cured. I am determined; I am strong, and fearless.*

"*If you hear a voice within you say 'you cannot paint,' then by all means paint and that voice will be silenced.*" Wrote my favorite painter, Vincent Van Gogh, who understood suffering, pain.

Zip lining is fun and the feeling of accomplishment so refreshing. As I head out through the little store, the owner's wife comes to me, introducing herself, handing me her card, and asking me to let her know how I am doing. She gives me a hug, and I proceed to the door, where the owner stands and says, "My daughter has something for you." The young woman hands me a CD with the pictures from the zip lining experience and gives me a hug, wishing me good luck. I turn to leave, and now I see that the owner and the two instructors are by the door, ready to each give me a hug. I leave humbled by the demonstration of care and love.

On the drive back home, driving by the beautiful and tranquil pastures, the tears roll down my face. I am not sad. I am not scared. I'm grateful for all I've experienced on this Sunday, finding it hard to comprehend that tomorrow I will be heading to Mayo for tests to see how The Dragon is responding to the treatment.

Spontaneously, I have an urge to stop by a small park before going home, to get on the swing. I *fly* a little high but I don't reach the stars. Even with company, I feel alone. I play a song on my phone... my heart weeps silently. How I wish to be hugged, but there are no arms around me.

"Celebrate what you want to see more of." — Tom Peters

St. Patrick's Day & Celebration

Always trying to lighten up the vibe within and around me, I put on green sweater, jacket and hat. I hand my sister a green shirt and scarf, explaining the Irish tradition we would be embracing on this rainy day.

As soon as we step into the clinic, people start to say "A true Leprechaun," "Love how you went all the way," and "You won't be getting pinched today," which is apparently what happens to people without green on.

The CT scan is quick, but the waiting for, and the MRI itself, are both long. I'm exhausted, thirsty and hungry, but amazingly relaxed and in the present, without worrying about the results I will receive tomorrow. I just realized I have been learning to be in the present, not dwelling on the past, which is gone, or the future, which isn't here yet.

And The Dragon has taught me yet another lesson!

March 18, 2014 - Treatment is Working. YES!!!

I have told my kids and sister: There can be five types of results, four of which we will take as encouraging. We'll be happy if the tumors disappear, a miracle I'd be delighted to see happen; if they shrink; if there are fewer of them; or if there is no change. The only bad news would be if there are more tumors or they are growing.

Dr. Attia walks in and does not make cheerful remark as usual. Hmm! But thank God, he goes on to say, "I did not get to see your results yet. We'll see them together." What a relief!

He puts the scans from February side-by-side with the new ones on the computer screen. For the first time I look at the dots indicating the tumors, the marks of The Dragon. He measures each lesion and keeps saying: "nice," as he detects reduction on each one. He does some calculations and concludes that there has been an overall 15% reduction in the size of the tumors, which is considered, by the book, stable condition, but he sees it as an improvement. I take the latest conclusion and CELEBRATE! Andrea and Amanda are with me. I record two videos and post on Facebook to share the good news with all the people who have been praying for me.

With gratitude in my heart, I thank all Gods and the Universe, as I close my eyes. Amen!

March 22, 2014 – Possibility of a Meaningful Project Brings Joy

I meet with Jennifer from the meditation center, one of those people who appeared in my life and are still here, in my heart, and on the chair next to mine. We are discussing turning my diary into this very book, and this brings life and joy to my being. She believes in this project, which infuses me with happiness, and gives some meaning and purpose to this, at times unbearable and still hard to believe, journey.

"Perhaps the butterfly is proof that you can go through a great deal of darkness, yet become something beautiful." — Unknown

Comfortable Bald; I Am Who I Am

I have borrowed all my daughter's hats, I have gotten four wigs and several fun-looking headbands, and I wear them all. But I feel the most comfortable when my head isn't covered and has only a cheerful band decorating it.

I can proudly say that my hair didn't, and its lack doesn't, define me. I am who I am, the unseen part of me, who is shown through actions and feelings.

During the past few weeks my sister, who is a photographer, clicks pictures of me as we share treasured moments at cafés, parks, and walks. We have fun and I feel so comfortable with my bald head. This morning we walk to the Jaffe's for breakfast. I think: I don't feel naked; I feel like myself.

March 24, 2014 – Third Round of Chemo Starts

The third round of chemo starts. Two friends from Brazil are visiting and the time spent together, even at Mayo, is joyful. As chemo starts, however, I am very tired. Andrea reminds me: "Of course you are tired! You have not stopped at all since the very first day chemo started, one and a half months ago." That's true, I admit. Feeling okay, I have not wanted to waste any precious second. But today, exhausted, we turn off the light between nurses' checkups every 20 minutes, and close our eyes.

*"Some people come into our lives and quickly go.
Some stay for a while and leave footprints on our hearts.
And we are never, ever the same."* — Unknown

LONELINESS OVERTAKES MY HEART AND SOUL

March 25, 2014 – Now I Know: The Dragon Gives and The Dragon Takes Away

All I want is to enjoy the news that the treatment is working, to be infused with hope and joy. However, here comes unexpected sadness.

Some people have come into my life out of nowhere, becoming amazingly important to me as a person, independently of this journey. Deep connection was felt as they entered my heart. Never occurred to me they weren't here to stay. This week, however, I feel that one of these friends I value the most stepping aside. I have come to rely on each caring vibe and prayer I have received, each moment shared, and more. I remind myself that one of the lessons to be learned by me in this lifetime, is to be alone without feeling lonely, and without much of a choice, I start to grieve my loss.

As the day ends, I'm so sad. I can't help but to blame the Dragon for it and at this moment of pain, I hate cancer. My heart hurts deeply and I cry, I cry, I cry.

March 26, 2014 – Another Down Day

It is hard getting up today and sadness lingers all day. Being added to the grief of the previous day is the fact that my sister leaves for Brazil tomorrow. I already feel a void. She has been right by my side for the past two months, sharing every laughter and tear with me. Time spent with her is priceless. Now she is leaving, as she should, to reenter the heart of her family. I can't help it but to feel deep sorrow, as my two best buddies go moving on with their lives... the fire of The Dragon burns my soul.

I understand that my own peace, strength, and soothing, needs to be found within, in the core of my true self, But at many moments, like this one, I just wish for a tight embrace to shield me from the pain of the fire of The Dragon.

March 27, 2014 – My Sister Leaves and More Unexpected News

I sneak out of the house early morning to get goodies for a special breakfast before Andrea leaves. I cut azaleas from my garden and make an arrangement, I light the candles, and all five of us sit together. The kids are going to miss her too, as I know they have leaned on her for emotional support during this painful period. We have a cheerful morning and then comes the good-bye.

I feel okay, somehow, until later when I get a call from my gynecologist's office informing me that my PAP smear came out abnormal. Here come the tears pouring down again, and this time I beg God: *"Please let me be healthy. Let me live. No more growth please. No more dragons."*

I call a friend, but there is no answer... less available for me now. I feel devastated and alone. Where is my ground? Where is my hope? Where are you?

*"If you feel gloomy inside, try wearing a purple wig.
Some will smile and their happy energy will reflect
back at you."* — Patricia Moreira-Cali

APRIL FOOL'S DAY, A YEAR SINCE THE FIBROID GREW, MY PURPLE WIG & NEW FRIENDSHIP

I am aware that this day last year brought concerning news that unleashed a series of events leading to acknowledgment that a certain Dragon had made its way into my body. However, the energy of the day goes to the trip to Mayo and to meeting a new angel.

At 7:30 a.m. I am being picked up by Ana, a beautiful soul I am meeting face-to-face for the first time, and who is willing to spend 12 hours with me going for chemo. We have a mutual friend, who tried to introduce us two years ago when Ana moved to town, but it never happened. Around my birthday two months ago, she came out of nowhere, sending me comforting messages and making a donation to LMS Research Direct on my behalf. She is one of the "strangers-turned-angels" The Dragon has brought into my life. We become great friends, instantly.

Today I wear a purple wig and I am so happy I had the guts to, as it has brought smiles to so many at the Mayo Clinic. People approach me to say how good my "hair" looks, including two young women, also battling cancer and bald. One asks to take a picture with me and the other asks if the store where I got the wig had pink ones. I promise to check. (I got Apryle a pink wig and we have been friends since.)

It brings me such joy to make others smile, even more so here, at a hospital setting. The effect of the simple act of daring to wear a purple wig was like a mirror, having their laughter reflected back into my heart. What a simple joy!

In the spirit of April Fool's day, I decide to tell Dr. Attia that I was going back to Brazil and was quitting the trial. He looks serious and worried as he says, "Are you serious? Please tell me you are not serious." I say, "Yes, I am", but looking at his disappointed expression I just had to quickly say "April Fool's Day!" Oh, he looked relieved and we laugh. Later I try the same prank with Pam, the trial coordinator. She stops for a minute and says, "No, you are not dropping out." I say, "I am." She insists, "No you are not. I know you and you are not a quitter." She is right. I am not quitting. I am going for the cure, and for kissing The Purple Dragon good-bye.

April 2, 2014 – More Teasing by The Dragon or The Universe?

I head to the gynecologist's office, hopeful, as I have been told that the abnormal PAP smear is probably a false positive, and is probably showing benign changes on skin due to the chemo.

However, when the doctor uses the microscope she says, "Well. It's probably nothing, but there is a suspicious area, so I need to biopsy it." She then warns me that it is going to be painful — and so it was, very painful.

A strong painkiller did the job after a couple of hours, just in time to go to the oncologist's office for the Leunesta shot.

I end the day extremely exhausted. I go to bed early, but at midnight I am already awake. Like most nights, I find myself with headphones on, listening to guided meditation, into the night, and until morning light starts to shine. Why? The uncertainty of the pending results of another biopsy must be bothering me deep inside.

"I would be glad to forget about it, but it weighs on my memory like sins linger in guilty minds." — William Shakespeare

175

"Be happy in the moment, that's enough. Each moment is all we need, not more." — Mother Theresa

PICNIC, MIXED EMOTIONS & ANEMIA

I've heard that nature is our greatest teacher. Nature is life. I remember one day long ago, when my son was just a little boy, and he asked me a question I had not prepared myself to answer: "Mom, what is God?" The first thing that came to my mind as an answer was "God is nature." I have always felt a deep connection to "It" all in nature.

Here I am, by the margins of the beautiful Lake Alice, sitting on a blue Balinese cloth, under a brilliant blue sky, and in the company of a friend who has meant so much to me these last months.

I feel I am where I am meant to be, enjoying a moment of happiness, but wonder why the Universe is still letting me feel emotional pain deep inside, while I deal with The Dragon and the side effects of chemo. My hemoglobin has dropped greatly this week and the anemia is making me very tired, out of breath, unable to even go for a walk. But this doesn't hurt as much as the pain I feel in my heart. It has now been aching, silently, for a while. This has been a parallel journey, one not shared, but felt deep inside. No meditation has eased the sorrow. Why Universe, God? Why? And I hear only silence for an answer.

April 4, 2014 – Tea With an Old Friend and Down Again: Mixed Emotions

Here I am at Volta Café, waiting for a friend I haven't seen in two years. He texted, wanting to meet me, saying it's past the time for us to reconnect.

Within a couple of minutes, I'm holding his hands as he sobs, saying, "It's okay. I am fine." With tears flowing he say, "It's not fair. You are such a good person. I think of you every single day. You don't deserve this." I comfort him! Isn't that interesting? I'm the one comforting! I get to feel how The Dragon's fire reaches far and has affected the life of others around me. We share a heartwarming time together over tea and make a deal to meet regularly.

The rest of the day I feel that many friends who had been present initially, have pulled away. My treatment is weighting on them, they are uncomfortable being around me, probably feeling helpless. I am also dizzy as I move. I cry while discussing this with John, and he says, "This has been too hard for everybody." I feel emotionally lonely and my body feels physically exhausted. I lie with guided meditation on. I need help to "fly" away, to find peace in my heart.

April 5, 2014 – Farmer's Market and Great Chat

I meet Ana, who has become an amazing and caring friend; always present. We walk the market, buying flowers and organic vegetables for juicing. Then we meet her husband, another beautiful soul, for lunch and an effortless chat. Time flew and I find myself amazed by the amazing people The Dragon has made appear in my life, as others distance themselves.

I started the day thankful but as I lay my head on the pillow at the end of this Saturday, I feel so lonely, and I plead to the Universe: *"Please let me love and feel loved. Help me erase the pain within. If it was not meant to be, why let me taste what I have always longed for, just to have me feel it slip away, painfully. Is this about me learning to let go of fear of abandonment, of being alone? Please not now God, not when I feel so fragile."* But then I remember I have been told by more than a couple of people that The Dragon is about me resolving issues I have bottled inside over the years, and healing the emotional problems is the path to healing my physical body to health. *"So, tough it out Patricia, and keep on going,"* I tell myself.

April 6, 2014 – I Hike Again, Despite Anemia. Yeah! I Trick The Dragon.

I open my heart wider to feel the spiritual connections around me. I watch *Super Soul Sunday* for a while. It keeps my mind occupied and gives me hope to hear enlightened people talk about life, destiny, purpose, Earth school, and what lies beyond life.

How cheerful I am to have the physical strength to hike at San Felasco trail again. I have missed walking side-by-side with my inner traveler. The surroundings are so lush; the temperature is perfect, and the vibe light and joyful. As I pass through a certain log, my heart memories travel back in time, to a time when I felt embraced and blissful.

The Universe whispers in my ears and my heart listens. "Be patient, hopeful." Hope to have back what The Dragon has taken away? I certainly hope so.

April 8, 2014 – Hey Dragon! You Can't Catch Me.... Ha, Ha, Ha

My friend Jennifer drives me to Mayo and Amanda meets us there. The doctor says I look good and the blood test shows that my hemoglobin held on, not plunging down as I was warned. Yes! No need to consider blood transfusion. My body is holding on despite the insults of the chemotherapy. The Dragon is not putting me down and that is empowering.

I share the news with all my Facebook friends, as I have done at every visit to Mayo since the port was placed. I record videos in both English and Portuguese, and thank God, so far I have been able to report good news, while wearing a smile. Their prayers and support are nothing short of extraordinary. They infuse me with companionship and hope.

A LMS survivor writes to me, "With such a spirit and purple wig, you might trick The Dragon." "Good! I want nothing more." I reply with a smile.

"Courage is resistance to fear, mastery of fear
- not absence of fear." — Mark Twain

TWO MONTHS ON CHEMOTHERAPY

Wow! It's been 60 days since chemo started. It feels like a lifetime ago since I was carefree about The Dragon, since I was still working, counseling my patients, concerned about their health, and not mine. Yes, it feels like a long time ago. People say I look good and I don't feel I look bad, but I feel that I have aged inside over the last 70 days, since The Dragon woke up. However, I am not giving up, and for a walk I must go now, to admire and take in the beauty of life.

April 11, 2014 – Visit From My Nephew is Refreshing & Biopsy Results Upsetting

I start the day with meditation in bed for over an hour. By mid-morning I am receiving Reiki from my friend Cris. Her energy is so uplifting. I have come to rely on her for support and her push for me to move forward in my life, leaving behind baggage that holds me down.

I leave sleepy and energized at the same time, stop at a local supermarket for some organic produce, and head to the airport to pick up my nephew Rodrigo.

By mid-afternoon, I am in a parking lot when I get the much-waited call from my gynecologist with the biopsy result. She starts by saying, "The cells were not LMS," as this would be the worst-case scenario, and proceeds to say, "But they were pre-cancerous, unrelated to the LMS, and possibly due to the chemotherapy."

I feel disappointment and a pinch of anger. I keep quiet, just saying "Yes," as she says, "I wish I had better news, but we will keep checking with PAPs every six months." I hang up and tears appear once again. I say out loud: "Universe. When do I get a break? When? When?"

Back at home I share the news with Yannick, John, and Rodrigo. I cry, filled with disappointment; I have been working so hard on being positive, on creating healing vibrations, on believing that I can heal myself as I align with the true nature of it all. Don't I deserve to have results that show my body improving, instead of deteriorating? Yannick holds me. I feel his love.

Later on I pray and again focus on positivity, on believing I am healing and getting cured. I remember Sylvia telling me to focus on my CURE, in the present, and not on healing.

Someone posts a question for me on Facebook: "How can you keep on being so positive through this all?" I answer: "The other choice would give me despair. This one gives me hope. I believe that the Universe, God, is listening, and I am doing my part."

April 12, 2014 – Merging with Nature

I wake up and just want to be still, in a meditative state. So, I lie in bed with my eyes closed, and think of nothing in particular. Later, the memories of hikes and porch time sneak in; I miss those blissful moments. I miss the quietness, the companionship. Before sadness creeps back in, I get up, thankful that I am here to live another day.

Around mid-day, Rodrigo and I, head to the crystal clear Icheetucknee River, fed by pristine springs, to kayak with Joy and Eric. Going slowly paddling down stream, surrounded by Mother Nature's beauty, is like praying. There are manatees, here from the ocean, escaping the cold waters; and there is me, escaping the reality of The Dragon for a while, emerging in pure bliss. *I feel healthy, I feel well, and I feel alive. I am grateful for being here, for this moment, for this gift.*

As the day ends, I feel very tired, courtesy of the side effects of chemo, but I can't complain; I had a beautiful day.

April 13, 2014 – When Life Deprives Me of Color, I Go To The Indian Holi Color Fest to Get Colorful

When Amanda sent the invite to the Indian Holi Color Fest at the Hare Krishna Center, I said, "Count me in." At noon we are driving through the beautiful countryside.

The vibe is festive and so colorful, the temperature is perfect, and music is in the air. On each hour, there is a color throw, when all those carrying bags of bright colored powder throw the colors at each other. The result is a fun and colorful mess all over our bodies and clothing, head to toe.

I post on Facebook a clip I made at the festival. Some friends' comments warm my heart and humble my soul:

"One more time you are teaching us how to live."

"Patricia, throughout your journey, you have been coloring the lives of so many people. You are inspiring, you are light, you are color, and you are needed here on Earth. Congratulations and I ask that God always show you your way. I love you more and more each day."

Another day I finish with gratitude filling and coloring my heart and soul.

"We do not create our destiny; we participate in its unfolding. Synchronicity works as a catalyst toward the working out of that destiny." — David Richo

FINALLY UNDERSTANDING SYNCHRONICITY

I start yet another day doing guided meditation on healing, stress relief, and soul searching. I hear Dr. Chopra say "synchronicity happens when we connect with the cosmic mind, when we introduce intention in the field of all possibilities." That got my attention, and I now start to understand what synchronicity is, and that "it isn't coincidence", as Dr. Brian had told me. Now I can make sense of all the synchronicities that happen in my life, like when I have searched and ended up finding ill, impoverished children in need of help, in remote areas of the world. More of my soul questions are being answered, and I feel a certain relief.

I wish I could also understand how I have dreams of death, or near death, of people close to me, *while it is actually happening*. But, I remember Dr. Weiss telling me, "Try not to think with your left brain. You don't have to analyze everything. Follow your intuition. I can tell that you can see very deep." And so, I let go, accepting the mysteries of the unseen world, the spiritual world.

April 15, 2014 - Forth Round of Chemo Starts

It has been 65 days since chemo started, and here I am, ready for another round, and thankful that my body has been handling it so well. Everyday I pray thanking every healthy cell in my body, for tolerating the insults of the poisonous chemo aimed at The Dragon tumors. I hope that as I try to keep a healthy balance within my soul and spirit, my body does the same, finding a way to balance the necessary evil (chemo), with the strength needed to keep my healthy cells strong.

My oncologist was impressed, actually surprised, that my blood counts were so good, with hemoglobin going up and platelets normalizing. Well, I am celebrating, but no longer surprised. The doctor only looks at the effect of the medical therapy, while I now believe in the power of the prayers and positive vibes sent my way, and the ones from deep inside my being. Body, mind and spirit have been working together with the medical treatment, in a harmonious way, as they should. This is what I have learned to believe and embrace during this past year, journeying with The Dragon.

"I was always looking outside myself for strength and confidence, but it comes from within. It is there all the time." — Anna Freud

BURNOUT AND LOVE: THE DRAGON WEARS OFF PEOPLE. THE JOURNEY BECOMES LONELIER.

A friend who works with terminally ill children had warned me that with cancer and long-term illness, sometimes people, including loved ones, may move in and out of your life. They may turn away, and move on with their lives, leaving the affected person feeling alone. Reasons for that can be many, ranging from lack of time to uneasiness and feeling helpless.

The reality on my end is that, no matter what the reason, it's hard to see friends moving on and away, one by one. For me, there is a duality in place: first I am encouraged to learn to receive help and support without guilt or shame; then, just I am feeling comfortable with that, I am supposed to tough it out and learn to move forward on my own. Hmm.

It has been 9 weeks since chemo started. Some days it seems like forever, and on others it seems like yesterday. The truth is that it is still fresh, and to hear one of my closest friends say that my treatment may take five years (I intend to see the Dragon take a hike, away from me, much sooner than that), that I have to do it on my own, that people have their on lives, et cetera, was painful. I understand and accept this reality, but to have had it thrown at me, to the tone of a bitter voice, was hard, very hard. The harsh voice also saying that I cannot expect to have people cook for me, referring to the Meal Train that was organized for me by my dear friend Joy, was upsetting.

I didn't ask for it, but I accepted it humbly, as part of the lesson in receiving. Shame and humiliation also surfaced.

I can truly say that I was not ready to hear such unnecessary accusations. I didn't have to hear what I already knew and I have been trying so hard to accept. It has been only 2 months, and this new phase is still fresh and very tough to endure. The tears come pouring down again, very strongly. I feel devastated.

When loved ones feel overwhelmed, they should just step aside, and not pour their frustrations and expectations on the person dealing with cancer... in this case, me.

Another person I love deeply has made all sorts of excuses not to meet up with me lately. My hairless head, I feel, triggered the pulling away. It hurts; I miss the times shared, but I have no choice but to accept the reality as it is. Everyone has the right to decide and choose what is good for him or her, I understand, but I suffer nonetheless.

The painful lesson to be learned is, that in the end, deep down, the journey with The Dragon is ultimately a solitary one, on so many occasions. Cancer burns out people. This is the truth I feel in this moment. Strength has to be found within. I must find it on my own, somehow.

April 19, 2014 – As Some Doors Close, Others Open

An amazing thing is that when some doors close, others open, sometimes by people you least expect. Feeling the love and support of people who were mere strangers just weeks ago, has been mind-blowing. Some are physically present, while others are far away, even in other countries, yet they make themselves present, filling some of the void.

But no one can substitute another. Feeling happy about new friends does not take the sorrow of losing old ones. However, I feel blessed to be able to say that there have been more people coming into my life, than leaving it. How wonderful is that?

April 20, 2014 – Easter

It's Easter Sunday. I drop off some chocolate eggs on friends' doors, without knocking, and then, a void. I walk through the deserted streets and find them so strange. I never wandered the streets on Easter Sunday before. This is the first time I don't have people over or get invited somewhere. Everyone is inside, gathering; I am walking with Ziggy, just the two of us. A little sadness sneaks in. Later I meet up with a Jewish friend. At least she has a reason not to be invited somewhere, I think, with a smile. We walk through her lovely neighborhood and I contemplate getting a studio where I can retreat to, to let go of fear of living alone, to meditate without interruption, and to simply be at this time of transitions. I want to make a clearing on the dense forest of my life, a space to heal, and let myself be, by myself, alone, yet without feeling lonely. Yes, I will get a space and turn it into my sanctuary, where I can go to listen to the voices within, and the revealing silence of the Universe. As for the criticism that probably will come from some, well, I will ignore the "editors" as they appear. This is my life! Now, that's empowering.

Just as we are walking through this lovely tree-lined street, I tell my friend that "If I could choose a place in this neighborhood, I'd love it to be on this street." Just then she remembers that a person she knows might be interested in renting a furnished studio behind her home. She doesn't know where the house is but she calls and leaves a message about my interest. (Later I visited the place and rented the studio. Guess where it was located? Yes, on the lovely street I just mentioned. Coincidence? Synchronicity!)

April 22, 2014 – Facing the Emotional Pain of a Loved One is Heartbreaking

I arrive from the double-chemo treatment day very tired and hungry. I just have time for a bite and I am called in for a family talk. I hear that one family member is coping with it all in unhealthy ways. I don't have much physical energy or much emotional strength to spare. I feel numb; it's hard to react. Tears come; decisions are made without much input from me. The sadness cuts through my heart.

I hug my child; I say "I love you" and that "We are all going to be okay." As I'm hugged back, I hear an apology, and then, "I am going crazy in this house, Mom." At this moment, I want to hate The Dragon, but I do not find hate in my heart; I opt for hope that I will be okay; we are all going to be okay, and will survive this journey stronger.

But 2:00 a.m. comes, and I'm still awake. I am still writing. I may be scared that the thoughts will hit me too hard if I close my eyes, despite all the meditation and relaxation techniques I have learned. However, just now, I decide I can't run from reality, and I need to believe I can engage in positive affirmations until my mind and soul believe them. And so, I am going to put the computer down and focus on looking forward to another day of happiness and good health, for me, my children, and us all.

I eventually fall asleep.

"What lies behind us and what lies before us are tiny matters compared to what lies within us." — Ralph Waldo Emerson

APRIL 23, 2014 – ONE YEAR ANNIVERSARY OF MY JOURNEY WITH THE PURPLE DRAGON

A year ago today, with a serene but intuitive heart that whispered to my ears that something wasn't right, I entered a room and heard the dreaded words Cancer, Sarcoma, and Leiomyosarcoma. The Dragon was introduced to me as the ferocious enemy that had entered my body without my awareness. From that point on my life was to change course forever.

Today, I drive to Moosewood Café, in a tiny town near by, where I have enjoyed many peaceful moments during the past year. I am alone. Wait. I am actually not alone. *"We are never alone"*, I have learned. I am in the company of the Universe and my own self. I order a latte and sit on the back porch. The cat I have seen many times comes near. I smile, thinking of all the *bizarre*, and *surreal* experiences I lived during the past year, many involving cats. My eyes gaze around the lush surroundings and as they meet the giant oak trees, I whisper to them, "You are all so old, yet you keep on living. I am not old, I don't feel old, but The Dragon is threatening my life. I so want to keep on living, to grow old, just as you oak trees."

Sipping the warm coffee, I ponder on the happenings of the past 365 days of my life, journeying with The Dragon.

My world crumbed down in a split second a year ago, and has been re-emerging, little by little, ever since. Much has been felt, much has been lived, and much has been learned. I have changed; hopefully I am wiser, or at least on the path to be wiser. I remember assertively telling my patients with diabetes: "You can be on the driver's seat of your health, but if you had a diagnosis of cancer, there wouldn't be anything you could do." Well, and here I am, with cancer. I guess one of the life lessons in store for me was to learn differently, and admit that I was wrong.

A diagnosis of cancer, even of the rare LMS type, requires *a lot to be done by the patient*, including *being patient*. First hand, I have learned that I could, and needed, to learn to take charge of my own emotional and spiritual self. I could care for my body more, giving it the rest, physical activity, and nutrients it needed to sustain the treatment, and to emotionally cope with the reality of the cancer diagnosis. I could find ways to conquer fear, embrace courage, and establish peace within, by nurturing my true essence, *the one thing* that never dies, my soul, my inner spirit.

I realized that The Dragon couldn't be my enemy, as it represents what is inside my heart and spirit that needs to be changed, for my own soul growth and healing. So I have partnered with The Purple Dragon, embracing it as my companion for the time being, but with the goal, of course, to see it gone far away from my body and life, when the right time comes.

In many ways, having to rely primarily on emotional and spiritual growth can be frustrating, particularly initially and at times of set backs, like when metastasis shows up.

As a person of science and research, where was the proof that surrendering and learning to trust the Divine Order, Intelligent Energy, The Universe, God, could lead to healing and cure? It was nowhere to be found. Of course I have heard of many miracles and I have wanted them for me too, but again, how can I know if I will be granted such a divine privilege? Well, I can't know. And so I learned that I must embrace *the unknown*.

Time reading, listening, and learning from spiritual leaders, and especially from people who have been where I am now and have come out of it as strong survivors, have given me hope. Living my "weird coincidences" has shown me there is *something else* out there, some invisible Source capable of the strangest things, and so, why not capable of curing me?

Relaxation, meditation, yoga, time on the trails, at the tree house, with Ziggy, and within, have shown me how to slow down, ruminate less, and let go more. I am learning to be patient, very patient, since healing takes time. I must trust that my cure is possible and will happen. Cancer appears when cells forget how to die. Well, I now believe that the power of the prayers, together with the medical treatment I am receiving, will teach the Dragon cells how to die.

There are hidden lessons to be learned from this all, and I must go through all of these experiences for now, to grow as a person and spirit. I have been practicing the difficult task to focus on today, on the now, on the present moment, not dwelling on the past, which is no longer here and can't be changed, or the future, which although can be shaped by my actions of today, still isn't here, and inherently has uncertainties. There are no guarantees in life, so I move on learning to shut up my rational left-brain and to trust my intuition, my gut feelings, and the flow of my life.

The helplessness I felt about the diagnosis of cancer has been fading away, as it should. What I strive for, day after day, is empowering myself to believe that I am okay and I can trust that my body can and will restore itself to good health. This is a much harder task than checking blood sugar with a device that gives you instant feedback about how you are doing. But again, there is *something I can do* to influence the outcome of the cancer and my well being, and that feels good, washing helplessness away.

So, this is the last page of my journal, but not of my journey. I started with not only great fear of The Dragon and great sorrow in my heart, but also with ignorance about the true meaning of life and death. By no means I have come to fully understand the essence of life, but I feel closer to "the truth" about the reality of it all. Sadness still comes and goes, fear still pokes in, but I have detached from much illusion, and I feel mostly at peace deep within.

The journey with the Dragon has been a bumpy one, filled with ups and downs, gains and losses, but I am moving forward with determination, and I won't stop until I reclaim my good health and my freedom back.

My intuition tells me that much is still to be lived, witnessed, enjoyed, and accomplished in this soul journey of mine here on Earth. My passion and enthusiasm for life is more alive than ever. My desire to dance the dance of life is ignited. So, am I ready to check out of this lifetime? **NO WAY! ARE YOU LISTENING, THE UNIVERSE? NOT YET AND NOT FOR A LONG TIME.**

With love and wishes that you have found your own peace, or are searching for it, that you are in good health, and that you are fully embracing each precious moment you have, I will simply say "See you later," until the next chapters of my life are written.

Patricia

"No one can fix your life for you. You need to set out consciously to do it for yourself. You must trust what you know in your bones that your body is your ally and that it will always point you in the direction you need to go next." — Christiane Northrup, M.D.